For Heidi

CONTENTS

THE WHY AND HOW

In July 1970 a book called *Future Shock* appeared. It has since
sold over seven million copies around the world, an astounding sale,
considering that it does not deal with Hollywood or sex. It offers no
how-to advice or get-rich-quick schemes. It is a serious work of
social analysis and criticism which has left a deep mark on readers in
every walk of life. The very phrase "future shock" has entered the
daily vocabulary and now appears in many dictionaries.

In 1980, the author of *Future Shock,* Alvin Toffler, published
The Third Wave—a book even more scholarly, analytic, and socially
committed than *Future Shock*. It, too, has become an international
best seller. It has broken sales records in Japan. It has been
translated into Danish, Hebrew, and Turkish, not to mention
French, German, and Spanish. It has been banned in Saudi Arabia
and published in Peking. A Polish translation was in progress when
martial law was declared in Warsaw. And at the time of the
interviews for this volume Mr. Toffler was working with Japanese,
Canadian, and American television crews to create a major TV
program based on *The Third Wave,* a show likely to carry Toffler's
messages to even wider audiences around the world.

These books, along with much of Toffler's earlier work, form a coherent body of interrelated ideas, and whether one agrees with them or not, they are clearly novel and provocative. They deal with change—its speed and directions. They synthesize information from fields as disparate as psychology, economics, technology, and history. They propose startling ways of thinking about the contemporary world.

It is not necessary to have read these earlier books to grasp the key ideas offered in *Previews and Premises*, a work unusual in both form and substance. It stands by itself, crammed with fresh material and intriguing, sometimes exasperating, insights.

Since Toffler's works *are* interrelated, certain allusions to *Future Shock* and *The Third Wave* are unavoidable. A few concepts outlined for the benefit of first-time Toffler readers, mainly in the opening two chapters, may already be familiar to those who have followed his work intimately.

Nevertheless, *Previews and Premises* reaches beyond Toffler's previous books to deal with sex roles, the politics of "mind workers," industrial policy, the philosophy of history, and other subjects only tangentially, if at all, referred to in his earlier work.

The key theme of *Future Shock*—a novel idea when that book first appeared—was that the acceleration of social and technological change has made it increasingly difficult for individuals and organizations to cope. It is not merely change to which we must in some way or another adapt, but acceleration, itself. Toffler argued that the very pace of change has effects quite apart from the direction and content of change. Writing of "the premature arrival of the future," he analyzed the processes of change in strikingly fresh terms and concluded that for democracy to survive it would have to become not only more pervasive and participatory, but more anticipatory as well.

The Third Wave complemented *Future Shock* and focussed on the directions of change, extending Toffler's system of thought and deepening its theoretical premises.

The main thesis of *The Third Wave* is that world industrial society, including both capitalist and socialist nations, is in a

Books by the Same Author

The Culture Consumers
Future Shock
The Eco-Spasm Report
The Third Wave
Previews & Premises

The Schoolhouse in the City (editor)
Learning for Tomorrow (editor)
The Futurists (editor)

PREVIEWS & PREMISES

2   3   4   5   6   7   8   9   10

PREVIEWS & PREMISES

BY ALVIN TOFFLER

An Interview with the Author of
Future Shock and *The Third Wave*

William Morrow and Company, Inc. • New York

1983

"general crisis." Toffler argues that the agricultural revolution of 10,000 years ago launched the first great wave of change in human society. The industrial revolution, beginning 300 or so years ago and bringing with it a tide of social and political strife, sent a second wave of change across the planet. And now, in Toffler's view, a new critical transition is upon us, as contemporary trends in technology, economics, politics, family life, energy use, and other spheres of life usher in a third civilizational rupture—a transition to Third Wave social forms.

These ideas have brought both controversy and recognition, *Future Shock* having been awarded the *Prix du Meilleur Livre Etranger* in France, a prize earlier given to works by Alexander Solzhenitsyn, W. H. Auden, and Lawrence Durrell.

A former visiting professor at Cornell University, Visiting Scholar at the Russell Sage Foundation, and member of the faculty of the New School for Social Research, Toffler has addressed groups in the U.S. Congress and the White House, the Japanese Diet, the British House of Commons—and may well be the only person who has ever delivered major addresses before the National Republican Governor's Conference and a Democratic National Convention on the same day. He has also spoken before the Institute of United States Studies in Moscow, the Japan Productivity Center in Tokyo, the National Physical Laboratory in New Delhi, the Institute of Politics at Harvard, as well as before scores of universities and corporations.

At each of these Toffler talks about the anachronistic character of contemporary social institutions, about the need for a revolution in the way we think, the way we conduct politics, and the way we organize our economy and family life, as well as about the trajectories of social development that make such revolutions highly likely. His views have deep political significance, yet Mr. Toffler claims that he is on neither the left nor the right of the contemporary political spectrum.

He decries our political party system and our government institutions as obsolete. He urges immense economic transformations. He supports the rights of women and of all minorities to equality and integrity of identity and purpose. Nonetheless, Toffler gives allegiance to no existing political parties or movements. He insists that the left/right axis of politics is increasingly obsolete in the high-technology nations, and that the main schisms that disrupt society occur along quite different fault lines.

Is he right? Are today's political movements anachronistic? Are the traditional conflicts of race, class, sex, age, or religion in our society subordinate to another set of conflicts with deeper roots and greater causal impact? Or, alternatively, are the waves of change Toffler describes themselves subordinate, playing themselves out in the context of more familiar political relationships and contradictions? Are the politics of both left and right obsolete, as he claims, or still relevant to the tasks of our time?

Does his focus on what he calls the "collision of waves" call attention to the primary fault lines in our society and thereby help us to understand and channel today's rapid social and political changes? Does his model offer us new weapons for the control of change? Toffler focusses our attention on a variety of important social trends. But does he simultaneously obscure other social relations and conflicts which will determine where these trends finally culminate, and which, if we are not diligent, will make our futures far darker than the Third Wave vision Toffler sees? To what degree can his novel analyses help us humanize the future?

Previews and Premises is based on a series of lengthy interviews initially suggested by members of South End Press. These interviews begin with the premise that our existing social institutions are dangerously inappropriate to the needs of our age and citizenry. They must be transformed—and soon—if we are to survive the turbulent times ahead. But what kinds of transformation are necessary or possible? Can our society survive on the basis of inequality and exploitation? Or will survival itself require a new level of equity, participation, and social diversity enriching all our lives? The answers to all such questions may turn on (a) what the primary determinants of contemporary change and its ultimate aims are; and (b) how we can, as citizens, understand and then intervene in these social processes.

When Alvin Toffler responded positively to our suggestion that we work together on this volume, we assigned an editor who began a series of wide-ranging conversations. We knew from the start there would be many disagreements. Toffler regards much of what passes for the left today as hopelessly anachronistic. His interviewer, by contrast, believes firmly in the importance of left politics and struggle. The book, however, could not be a debate—the point was not to try to resolve all differences, a naive hope to attach to such a limited process. Instead, the hope was to create a provocative exchange in which Toffler would enrich his past formulations, extend them to new domains, and, when the flow of the interviews warranted it, respond to critical questions rooted in a left-wing analytic perspective.

At this point, some of Toffler's readers may ask why an author with a world-wide audience, a heavy readership in the business community, and access to much larger publishing houses, agreed to such intensive interviews conducted from a political perspective he does not share.

The answer, according to Toffler, is that the project gave him an opportunity to deal with certain questions that arise from the left, and which are seldom asked of him by the mainstream press in the West. Toffler wanted to consider and confront questions having to do with such issues as ownership, class, political authority, racism, sexism, and, as he sees it, the severe weakness of Marxism.

Such questions are, of course, of crucial importance to all readers concerned about the fate of our society. They are questions all of us will have to face before too long.

South End Press's interest in the project is related. We felt that the treatment of these issues in the mainstream media—where they are dealt with at all—is often shallow. While the style of *Previews and Premises* is not directly confrontational, and disagreements between interviewer and author are not often pushed to irreconcilability, we believe the cross-fertilization of views is fruitful and that the project sets a useful precedent.

The book itself assumes an unconventional form.

The first part, entitled *Previews*, is devoted to Toffler's latest views on current problems: today's economic crisis, the future of work and unemployment, myths about Japan, and the strategies of other countries as they face the breakdown of industrial society. Toffler examines the prospects for capitalism and socialism, and tackles questions about the new role of women and minority groups in the fast-emerging society of tomorrow.

The second part of the book, entitled *Premises*, is quite different and also more personal. To help readers evaluate the underlying assumptions in Toffler's view of the world, we begin with a biographical section—what experiences in his background helped form his present unorthodox views? This is followed by a short history of futurism and, then, by a deep probe into Toffler's working methods. How does he organize his research? How does he synthesize disparate ideas and information into an integrated intellectual structure? How does he model change?

After our lengthy conversations, work on the voluminous transcripts began. This involved more than merely cutting and pasting, or the insertion of subtitles. As the work progressed, in addition to cutting and stylistic editing, Toffler began writing fresh new thoughts—new sections, questions, and answers were added—so that while formally retaining the structure of an interview, the resultant manuscript has been significantly extended and refined, much like any work of prose. The original transcript has served more as a general guide than as a source for verbatim quotation. We believe *Previews and Premises* will encourage readers—whether or not they agree with the particular views expressed—to reexamine afresh their own implicit previews of the future and their own underlying premises.

South End Press
Boston, Massachusetts

PART ONE
PREVIEWS

The test of a first-rate intelligence is the ability to hold two opposed ideas in the mind at the same time, and still retain the ability to function.

One should...be able to see that things are hopeless and yet be determined to make them otherwise.

The Crack-Up
F. Scott Fitzgerald

1 THE ECONOMIC UPHEAVAL

We are feeling the first tremors of an economic earthquake, and we had better prepare for it.

As we speak, the Western capitalist world is suffering higher levels of unemployment than at any time since the Great Depression of the 1930s. Communist nations like Poland and Rumania are virtually bankrupt. The Soviet economy is a shambles. World banking systems teeter on the razor-edge of collapse. And the ideas of our economists seem more remote from reality with every passing hour.

Nevertheless, the nature of the crisis is widely misunderstood. Many of our most basic economic concepts are obsolete. Neither conservatives nor liberals, neither the "right" nor the "left" have answers, because both are locked into anachronistic ideological commitments.

What is happening is not like a hurricane that sweeps across the landscape, leaving the earth itself unchanged. It is more like the beginnings of an earthquake. For the subterranean structure on which all our economics are based is now, itself, shifting, cracking. In our efforts to prevent a major collapse, we are dealing with surface phenomena rather than focussing on the deep-structure, where the really big changes are occurring.

—A.T.

■ You use the provocative word "earthquake" to describe what is happening, or beginning to happen, to our economy today. And it isn't the first time you've warned of massive impending changes in the economy. In *The Eco-Spasm Report*, which you published in 1975, you foreshadowed many of today's economic events. But neither in that book, nor in *The Third Wave*, do you suggest that today's crisis may actually benefit some people, while others walk the streets, lose their jobs, and see their welfare benefits slashed.

Some even argue that in the United States, the immediate crisis has been deliberately engineered. In this view, a dose of unemployment makes workers more pliant. Unions are put on the run, taking wage cuts. Women and minorities are forced to give up advances they've sought over the years. We become a less fair society as income differentials widen and the burden of economic crisis is borne unequally. Moreover, slashing welfare benefits forces workers to enter the job market at any cost, bidding down wages and accepting deteriorating work conditions. In short, enlarging the pool of unemployed means corporations can lower wages, increase productivity, and increase profits all at the same time.

□ That's one way of looking at it. But the same crisis is rolling across many nations at once. The idea that this was deliberately engineered presupposes a far higher degree of control than anyone in our society is capable of. Furthermore, it overlooks far more fundamental issues.

The press calls what is happening a recession. And when the recession hits you personally, it suddenly becomes no longer a "recession" but a "depression." I fully understand that. I understand that people are being hurt, and that it is always the little guy who is hurt worst.

But continually referring to this as a recession or a depression masks what's really happening. It focusses attention on the symptoms, not the causes.

During previous depressions, there were crises in the basic industries. Layoffs. Unsold inventories. Bankruptcies. Foreclosures. Major industries shut down.

But you seldom if ever saw powerful new industries rising up at the very same time.

Today the mass manufacturing industries—auto, steel, rubber, textile, the backbone of the traditional industrial economies—are in terminal agony. Belgian steelworkers, British autoworkers, textile workers in North Carolina and Japan are being laid off.

Yet, simultaneously, we see an explosive rise of electronics, computers, information, genetics, aerospace, environmental recycling, certain services, and alternative energy industries—all of these, admittedly with some ups and downs, are expanding.

What's happening is not a recession as such, but a restructuring of the entire technoeconomic base of the society. It's like an earthquake that throws up a new terrain. Unless that's understood, no tinkering with interest rates, taxes, wage and price policies, or trade relations can save us. Nor will strikes and demonstrations.

In short-hand terms, we're shifting from a Second Wave to a Third Wave economy. I'd go further than that....

■ Before you do, you ought to define your terms for those who haven't read *The Third Wave*.

☐ The terms are oversimplifications. But they help set today's changes into historical perspective.

In crude terms, we can say that, thousands of years ago, a wave of agriculturalization began. Nomads and hunters, fishermen and foragers became peasants. Villages sprang up. What we call "civilization" was born. For simplicity's sake, let's call that the First Wave of change.

Then, 300 years or so ago, a second wave of change began. Machines, mass production and consumption, mass media and mass education—a whole factory-based way of life replaced the old agricultural civilization over approximately a quarter of the globe. I call this spread of industrialization the Second Wave.

■ If the First Wave brought agriculture and the Second Wave brought industrial mass society, what is the Third Wave bringing?

◻ It's very hard to define the new revolution precisely because we are living in it. Just as a person born at the time of the industrial revolution might have been aware of the great changes taking place, but confused by their complexity, we are in the same situation. It appears to us as a great rush of seemingly unrelated changes.

It's the computer—but it's not *just* the computer. It's the biological revolution—but it's not *just* the biological revolution. It's the shift in energy forms. It's the new geopolitical balance in the world. It's the revolt against patriarchy. It's credit cards plus video games plus stereo plus Walkman units. It's localism plus globalism. It's smart typewriters and information workers and electronic banking. It's the push for decentralization. At one end, it's the space shuttle—at the other, it's the search for individual identity. It's flex-time and robots and the rising militancy of black and brown and yellow people on the planet. It's the combined impact of all these forces converging on and shattering our traditional industrial way of life. Above all, it's the acceleration of change, itself, which marks our moment in history.

To make sense of all these seemingly accidental or unconnected changes, we need powerful new models. That's what I tried to present in *The Third Wave*—a model that can help us identify the interrelationships among all these changes. But we also need new economic models. Because you can't begin to understand the economy until you relate it to these new forces. We are restructuring the economy because we are restructuring the entire civilization of which it is, after all, only a part.

■ What, in your opinion, is driving the economy downward today?

◻ Today's economic crisis has been blamed on low productivity. On lazy workers. On stupid management. On too much welfare. On inadequate investment. On the loss of the work ethic. It's blamed on Japanese imports. It's blamed on American interest rates. It's blamed on Arabs. Blacks. Jews. Migratory workers. Bloated capitalists. The Marxists insist it's the general crisis of capitalism—as though Marxist economies weren't in crisis, too.

None of these diagnoses fits the facts.

The central proposition of my work—as it affects economics—is that today's crisis is not a crisis of re-distribution, or of over- or under-production, or of low productivity (whatever that means), but a *crisis of restructure*—the breakdown of the old Second Wave, industrial era economy and the emergence of a new Third Wave economy that operates on different principles.

And Second Wave remedies—whether of the so-called left or right—only intensify the crisis.

■ Few would disagree that something new is happening. It isn't only an old-style capitalist crisis we are enduring, and a lot of our economic theories are obsolete, as you say. But for readers to assess your views, you need to be more specific. How does a Third Wave economy, as you call it, differ from a Second Wave economy?

□ I can outline the differences in short-hand form. But first we need to establish a frame of reference.

The changes I'm talking about are global—they affect many countries. And they are revolutionary—not in the narrow, political sense, but in the sense that they imply a comprehensive social transformation.

The crisis isn't capitalist or communist—it is *industrial*. Both capitalist and communist economies are teetering. Historically, the economy created by Second Wave civilization is approaching its terminal crisis. Even though we can still see them at work in places like South Korea, Brazil, or Mexico, the cultural and technological forces that created and spread industrialism are spent.

New forces are erupting onto the world scene, unleashing a new, a third wave of change.

THE SMOKESTACK AS RELIC

■ We need concrete examples.

□ Take mass production. Nothing was more characteristic of the industrial era. Yet we're already moving from a mass production, mass consumption economy to what I've called a "de-massified" economy.

In traditional mass manufacturing, factories pour out a stream of identical objects, by the million. In the Third Wave sector, mass production is replaced by its opposite: de-massified production— short runs, even customized, one-by-one production, based on computers and numerical controls. Even where we turn out millions of identical components, they are frequently configured into more and more customized end products.

The significance of this can't be overestimated. It's not simply that products are now more varied. The processes of production are themselves transformed. The smokestack—that symbol of the industrial, assembly-line society—is becoming a relic.

We still think of ourselves as a mass production society, yet in the advanced sectors of the economy, mass production is already an outmoded technique. And the idea that we can keep our old mass manufacturing industries competitive indefinitely is based on ignorance of what is actually happening on the factory floor.

The new technologies make diversity as cheap as uniformity. In fact, in many industries, it's customize or die. This is exactly the opposite of what was required in the Second Wave economy.

In fact, it is almost a dialectical return to pre-industrial, one-of-a-kind production, but now on a high technology basis.

And exactly the same trends are visible in the distribution system, too, where we see more and more market segmentation, direct mail targeting, specialty stores, and even individualized delivery systems based on home computers and teleshopping. People are increasingly diverse, and, as a result, the mass market is breaking into small, continually changing sectors.

This is a revolutionary fact: mass production and mass distribution are no longer "advanced methods." They are backward methods. The entire economy is de-massifying. This is a profound change, an historical change. It's the stage beyond mass society, and our conventional economists have hardly begun to notice it yet.

You can't deal intelligently with the issue of employment, or the issue of aggregate demand, or even the issue of government services, until this de-massification principle is taken into account. It is the most important shift in the character of the market economy since the industrial revolution. And it comes hand in hand with major changes in the "non-exchange," non-market economy as well.

We're also seeing an expansion of production for use, rather than exchange. The Third Wave economy is not merely de-massifying, it contains a significant and growing sector based on what I call "prosuming."

THE INVISIBLE PRODUCERS

■ Which is what, exactly?

□ Governments are discovering more and more that people don't like to pay taxes, and that they barter goods and services or "moonlight" on jobs that are off-the-books. The economists are making a big thing of this discovery, which naturally enough affects the tax system. This is what is called the underground economy. It's the uncounted part of the exchange system.

But something else is happening that is inherently more important.

People are actually producing more goods and services, not for sale, or even for barter, but for their own use. Not "petty commodity production," but, to be accurate, production for consumption by the producer. I call it "prosuming." It alters the relationship of the consumer to the production process. Today it takes the form of an exploding do-it-yourself market. Producers buy tools and materials from the marketplace, but then employ them outside the exchange system. Prosuming also takes the form of countless self-help groups.

And the service sector is absolutely riddled with examples of what might be called "co-production"—in which the consumer or a third party plays a role in production.

The most familiar example of co-production is the self-service gas station. Once the station attendant pumped the gas while the motorist sat in the car. Now at many stations the motorist gets out and pumps the gas. The buyer has taken on a function once performed by the seller. The end-result is the same, but the consumer has co-produced the result.

As we shift toward information and services, the lines become blurry, indeed. Another example: a government agency announces a program to eliminate an agricultural blight. Success depends on farmers applying a new method. A television station (at no cost to the agency) broadcasts a program showing how the new method works. The TV station provides the necessary information. (Without this service, the government agency might have had to spend money for leaflets or extension agents to visit the farms.) The TV broadcast, in this case, might justifiably be seen as part of the production process itself, and the TV station as a co-producer of improved crops.

Across the board, consumers and third parties are taking on tasks externalized by producers, and the old clear distinctions fade as a result.

The question of who supplies what information to whom at what cost, the question of what tasks are externalized by producer to consumer, and the production of goods and services by the consumer for his or her own use, outside the market, become increasingly important as we shift out of an industrial economy. They affect the very definition of productivity, itself. The economy is riddled with millions of unacknowledged, invisible producers.

So, in addition to de-massifying the economy, we are also shifting the roles of producers, consumers and third parties. The entire system is being restructured without our noticing it.

CUTTING-EDGE INDUSTRIES

■ And where do the new industries fit into your Third Wave economy?

□ By replacing Second Wave mass manufacturing industries with new, Third Wave industries, we are doing more than a simple substitution. The new industries are radically different from the old.

■ There are new products, to be sure; many new techniques, of course; but also the same old motives and familiar social relations. Why can't these "Third Wave" industries be seen as essentially more of the same—new extensions of old forms?

☐ Because they differ in a thousand ways. The kind of products. The kind of people in them. Their organizational structures. Their style and culture. And at the most profound level—the level of knowledge—they represent a fundamental break with the past.

Second Wave industries used brute force technologies—they punched, hammered, rolled, beat, chipped and chopped, drilled and battered raw materials into the shapes we needed or wanted. These basic manufacturing processes were analogs of human sensori-motor activity. Even the cave man chipped and chopped. Industrial society created machines that extended human muscle power and sensory acuity.

The Third Wave industries operate at an altogether deeper level. Instead of banging something into shape, we reach back into the material itself and reprogram it to assume the shape we desire. We can create wholly new materials. We operate at a molecular and sub-molecular level. Instead of inventing simple-minded machines to chop or punch or hammer things repetitively, we endow tools with intelligence so that they can adjust rapidly to changing circumstances and turn out individualized products economically.

And, if there is any analog to human effort here, it is to mind, rather than muscle. Instead of extending brute force, the new technologies extend human mental power.

The result is that the new Third Wave industries have sharply different social, organizational, cultural and environmental implications. They no more resemble the displaced mass manufacturing industries than a laser beam resembles a battering ram.

■ Which, in your judgment, are these new industries?

□ The Third Wave industries range from electronics, lasers, optics, communications, and information to genetics, alternative energy, ocean science, and space manufacture, ecological engineering and eco-system agriculture, all reflecting the qualitative leap in human knowledge which is now being translated into the everyday economy.

When you relate these new technologies to the new de-massified production and distribution processes, and also to the altered roles of producers, consumers, and third parties in the economy, you begin to glimpse the depth of the restructuring now taking place.

And we haven't seen anything yet. It is only when they are linked together in convergent systems (as is just beginning to happen in, say, computers and communications) that we will begin to appreciate the full power of the Third Wave technological base. Second Wave economic structures cannot contain these new forces.

The sudden arrival of these new industries onto the world scene at this point in history helps explain why so many national economies are in crisis.

REGIONS VERSUS NATIONS

■ Later we can return to how—or whether—these new technologies augur new social and economic relationships. But for now let's look at another of your controversial arguments. In your writings you have also suggested that national economies as such may be outmoded. Why?

□ That's yet another dimension of the restructuring now going on. During the age of industrialism, we went from small-scale enterprises serving local communities to bigger and bigger companies operating on a national scale. This was made possible by the new industrial technologies, by new transportation and communications systems that tied whole nations together, by mass media that served the national distribution machinery, and so forth.

Then, in the past few decades, we saw the rise of the multinational corporation. As the power of technology leaped to a new stage, and the international banking system reorganized itself to service giant, multinational corporations, as computers and new communications systems were laid in place, a higher and higher percentage of world production was done for multinational rather than national markets.

But little attention has been paid to the opposite trend that has been gathering momentum at the same time: the shift from national to smaller-than-national production. Today, when we look at Kyushu in southern Japan, or Scotland, or Quebec, or Texas, we find regional economies that have become as large and complex as national economies were only a few decades ago.

Because of cultural and technological trends, it is now possible to produce certain goods for regional or even local markets that until now could only be supported by national markets.

California has become the seventh or eighth largest economy in the capitalist world. New York State, Texas—from an economic point of view, these are giants. These are national markets, for all practical purposes, but they are trapped and restrained by a web of laws, taxes, regulations, and central bank measures that were designed for, and administered at the national level. More and more, these regional economies will break out of national economic frameworks and demand to go their own way.

And they are growing more divergent. This helps account for rising regionalism in culture, from poetry to cuisine, and, of course, in politics.

■ But surely, most secessionist movements, for example in Canada or Western Europe, are primarily cultural.

□ Of course, we should never underestimate the cultural component—like the battle over language in Belgium and Canada, or the ethnic and historical differences in France and Spain. But the more these regions become economically viable—or potentially viable— the more autonomy they demand. Scotland has North Sea oil.

Quebec, rightly or wrongly, thinks of itself as able to sell hydropower to New England.

The key is that, whether we call these units "regions" or "nations" or whatever, they are diverging, rather than converging. And that means that managing their economies centrally, from the national level, whether in Washington, Tokyo, Paris, London—or Moscow, for that matter—will become more and more difficult.

The old tools of national economic policy, like national taxation or central bank regulation of money supply, let alone central planning, are crude, indiscriminate instruments designed for a mass production, goods-oriented economy. And they were designed for a nation-based economy, not an economy in which multinational and regional (or even sectoral) economies are becoming more important than the national economies. They're just too coarse, too insensitive and unselective to deal with a de-massified economy.

That poses a profound problem for both the capitalist central banker and the socialist nationalizer. I call it the "adrenalin problem." The example I often use to illustrate the problem is the hospital. Our economy is suffering from many different strains and ills. But our economists and governments, whether they are monetarist, welfare statist, or socialist, are like doctors who make hospital rounds and then prescribe the same medicine for all the patients—adrenalin for everyone—whether the problem is a broken leg or a brain tumor.

Nowadays uniform national policies cause increasingly dangerous side-effects in regional or local economies. They may also send unanticipated ripples through the global economy.

THE IMPACT OF INFORMATION

■ So far, you have defined the new economy in terms of demassification, co-production, and regionalism. What about the "information society" everyone hears so much about?

□ Certainly, there's been a well-documented increase in white collar and service jobs as manufacturing has declined—though whether that process will continue, as office automation spreads, is a question. But I'd like to point out certain implications of the information society that most economists have missed. They are crucial to understanding the restructuring of the economy.

To begin with, why *is* there an information revolution? I've never heard a good explanation of its causes.

I'd like to suggest that it is tightly connected with the de-massification of the economy and the rising level of social diversity. Without going into theoretical detail, I would argue that the more the mass society fractures, the more de-massified we become, the more the economy becomes differentiated, the more information must be exchanged to maintain integration in the system.

So, for me, the information revolution not only makes possible, but is also fed by, the break-up of mass production and mass marketing. The two are different sides of the same electronic chip.

De-massification is one of the key causes of the information revolution. And the result is revolutionary.

■ Why revolutionary? Do you expect changes in the basic distribution of wealth and power to result simply from our using new information technologies?

□ Fundamental shifts in power and the distribution of wealth will inevitably occur. But not necessarily along the fault lines we normally monitor. The term revolutionary is justified because the new facts turn our old assumptions inside out.

Marx, for example, spoke of the "labor theory of value." It might be useful to elaborate an "information theory of value." By that I mean that, if we look at the traditional "factors of production"—land, labor, and capital—they are all finite. If I use an acre of your land to grow wheat, you can't simultaneously use the same acre. If I use your labor or capital, you can't use it at the same time. Moreover, labor can be fragmented, homogenized, and tightly regulated. But information is different.

There was always an information component in production. Even making a stone axe requires some know-how. And Marx recognized the importance of knowledge when he spoke of "socially necessary labor time" as something that changed with each advance in technology. But what has happened now is that information is becoming an ever more crucial factor, and it is different from the other factors—even dialectically opposite.

If you use a piece of information, I can use it too. In fact, if we both use it, the chances are improved that we will produce more information. We don't "consume" information like other resources. It is generative.

That, by itself, knocks hell out of conventional economic theories.

And, as if that weren't enough, consider the impact of information on the division between work and home.

The information revolution opens the way to transferring millions of jobs from centralized offices and factories into neighborhood work centers and even into homes. Once again, a direct reversal of one of the basic trends of the industrial revolution.

THE BACK-TO-THE-HOME MOVEMENT

■ Ignoring for now the possibility that these information breakthroughs may also open the door to less benign possibilities, is this what you mean by your idea of the "electronic cottage"?

□ Yes. When *The Third Wave* was published in 1980, that was regarded as a crazy idea. Two years later, *Business Week* reported that the idea is "starting to have a significant impact on labor relations planning" and some U.S. experts were already forecasting that 15,000,000 jobs could be performed at home by the mid-1990s. If that were to occur, it would have an enormous impact on the structure of the economy.

■ But couldn't work at home easily involve harsh piece-work procedures as well as a loss of the social factor people can enjoy on the job? Don't people need the sense of belonging and social interchange with other people? If workplaces were more humane and participatory, wouldn't the social element become a positive attribute? Moreover, some people would question whether management will let it happen, since it may mean the loss of close supervision and control.

☐ Those criticisms seem to me to cancel one another out. One suggests that bosses won't let employees work at home because they will be unsupervised—that controlling the workers will be too difficult. The other suggests just the opposite: that the machines will supervise the workers even more closely than is possible today.

The truth will probably depend heavily on the specific nature of each job, and also on the degree to which those in the electronic cottages organize themselves for self-protection.

Remember—and this point is usually overlooked—these aren't illiterate workers just off some feudal manor. They are sophisticated workers, and they may, in fact, be able to use their home computers, video and telecommunications links to organize new networks, "electronic guilds," new professional associations, and other forms of self-managed or self-protective groups. New forms of collective action will be possible, too. Someday we may see "electronic strikes." I'd worry more about the conditions of workers left behind in the offices and factories.

Instead of resisting home-work, as unions typically do, the unions ought to be thinking imaginatively about how to set humane standards and how to help home-workers self-organize.

And as to socializing on the job, that question pops up every time the term electronic cottage is mentioned.

Of course, everyone needs social contacts. And, of course, we could make these more meaningful than they are today in most plants and offices. But people have *always* needed social contact with others—and they got plenty of it long before offices and factories existed. Do we really think the majority of the human race that never sets foot in a factory or office is lacking in human contact, friendship and emotional warmth?

If anything, the reverse is true. Factory production destroyed, rather than enriched, many human ties. We used to criticize the social alienation of factory life. Now, just when an alternative suddenly becomes historically possible, the factory is held up as an ideal! It's absurd.

Right now, millions of commuting workers come home at night and flop down in front of a television set. That's an isolating experience. But people who work at home are far more likely to want to *leave* home in the evening or as soon as work is done. They want to see people, to socialize, to meet friends, to engage in community activity.

Today, because of commuting, many of our suburbs are social graveyards. The electronic cottage, far from isolating people, may bring fresh life to these communities as home-workers fan out at night to participate in the local theater group or church or political party or fraternal organization. If home-workers have fewer social ties in the office or factory, they may have much *closer* ties with their families and communities.

So I don't buy the notion that the electronic cottage means social isolation. It's too simple. I also don't believe we'll see a single uniform pattern. Some people will, no doubt, work a few days in the office and a few days at home. Some will go to the office for three weeks, then come home for one week to actually get the job done away from the phone calls and distractions of the office. I think there will be as many patterns as there are industries and products and work-tasks. And, by the way, it opens wholly new options for handicapped people and older people who are now forced into "non-productive" roles in society. I think it could create new, stronger family and community bonds.

It's true, women have been banging at the doors of the labor market, some out of dire economic necessity, others simply to escape an empty home. And that will, no doubt, continue to be the case. But bear in mind that the home itself changes, becomes less vacuous, less lonely, when it becomes the center of work, education and other family activities.

What's more, there are some 350,000 home-operated businesses in the United States owned by women. They run the gamut from services like nurseries and caterers to computer programming, architectural design or management consulting.

That's been a little undiscovered island in the economy, accounting for literally billions of dollars of business. And it's operated without any technological support. Now, suddenly, give it cheap computers, cheap telecommunications, video equipment and the like, and I believe it will explode.

Stop for a moment to look at the whole issue in historic perspective. The industrial revolution wrenched paid work out of the home and put it into factories and offices. That transformed society. It altered family life. It led to the transfer of education out of the home. It created the whole ridiculous pattern of mass commuting. It shaped our cities and our lives.

This suggests that the transfer of any significant proportion of work back into the home would also carry strong changes with it.

■ But what makes you so confident all this is going to happen?

□ No one can be sure of anything. But look at the pressures building up.

To start off, there is the long-term rise in the cost of energy. Every time the cost of transportation goes up, employers are compelled to increase wages accordingly. They may resist for a time, but, if they want their workers to show up, they eventually have to provide a transportation subsidy. It's built right into the wage structure.

Next, the entire system of commuting implies hidden costs. Companies that bring employees to a central location wind up paying more for real estate; they pay higher taxes, maintenance costs and salaries. They often have to provide cafeterias, locker rooms, and, in suburban locations, parking facilities—there is a whole infrastructure that supports the commuting process. All of these costs have been skyrocketing.

By contrast, as we all know, the costs of telecommunications and computing and video equipment, and other tools for "telecommuting" are plummeting. So you have two powerful economic curves about to intersect.

But even more important, we all worry about "productivity." And there are all kinds of schemes to improve it (however "it" is defined).

Without doubt, the single most *anti-productive* thing we do is to shift millions of people back and forth across the landscape every morning and night. A waste of time, of human creativity, of millions of barrels of non-renewable fuel, a cause of pollution, crowding, and God knows how many other problems! And the cost to the workers is even greater.

We worry about the human effects of home-work. But how human is commuting itself? For most workers commuting is actually an unpaid part of the job—a deadening, miserable routine in which most workers are socially isolated for hours at a time! Most people hate that part of their work-lives. Just ask them if they'd like to be liberated from it!

Commuting was essential when most workers had to handle physical goods in factories. Today, as the Third Wave industries expand, many workers travel to work to handle information, ideas, numbers, programs, formulas, designs, and symbols—and it's a lot cheaper, not only in money terms, but in terms of energy savings, to move the information to the worker than the worker to the information.

There are all kinds of parallel cultural and value shifts, as well, that support the idea. The new emphasis on revived family life. The decentralist push—nothing is more decentralized than working at home. The resistance to forced mobility—you don't have to move your family when you change your job. Environmental concern— nothing pollutes more than centralized production. Etc., etc.

Add all these pressures together, and you understand why this transfer of certain jobs into the home seems so likely. Moreover, you have to see this development not by itself, but as linked to the de-massification of production and distribution; decentralization toward the regions; the rising importance of information; the appearance of wholly new, unprecedented industries; the break- down of national tools for economic regulation or management; the rising importance of co-production and non-market production—and many other mutually reinforcing changes.

We are restructuring the economy on all these fronts at once. No wonder our economic vocabulary is outdated. No wonder our economic maps no longer reflect the terrain. A new Third Wave economy is taking shape.

■ If one were to accept your argument that a basic restructuring of the economy is taking place, there would still remain questions of social justice, equity, and humanity. This transformation is likely to take decades to complete. What about the meantime?

What's going to happen to the millions of workers who are caught in the dislocations? What happens to the poor? To women and minorities? To the elderly? And don't we run the risk of creating an even less democratic society, with a handful of educated people doing the well-paid work, and the rest living powerless lives doing menial work? What will prevent your Third Wave economy from putting intellectual, managerial, and scientific types in a new driver's seat, with the rest of us still stoking the engine—sweaty, tired, and bossed about as ever?

☐ To answer that question, we first need to explore the future of work.

2 THE FUTURE OF WORK

Who will work? What is work? Are we heading toward some dystopian fantasy in which two percent of the population use robots and perform all the paid work, while 98 percent do none?

In the late 1950s and early 1960s, the introduction of factory automation was greeted with forecasts of massive unemployment. Arguing that full employment would no longer be possible (or even desirable), certain economists urged a minimum guaranteed income for all, irrespective of whether they held a job or not.

The fears of the fifties and sixties abated, however, as the composition of the workforce shifted. In many countries, while manufacturing jobs grew scarcer, millions of new white collar and service jobs opened up.

Today there are renewed fears about rising technological unemployment, and, with automation spreading most rapidly in the office, it is unlikely that the white collar sector will take up the slack again.

Where will jobs come from this time?

How will work itself change?

—A.T.

■ You say a major restructuring is taking place in our economic life—along with equally powerful upheavals in social institutions and values. But the question still remains, who will benefit from it?

Given technological change, what kinds of changes in institutional relations will take place? Aren't there conflicts of interest at work here among capitalists, managers and professional types, workers, men, women, whites, and blacks? Nearly 30,000,000 people are out of work in the Western countries. Other millions spend their lives in soul-destroying work—and are told they are lucky. The threat of an even worse economic crisis looms large. And in much of the rest of the world, the situation is unimaginably worse.

Yet you seem optimistic, in spite of it all. Why?

□ I am by no means an optimist when it comes to the short term. I think we may be only millimeters away from an even bigger economic disaster. I've been saying this since at least 1975, when I published *The Eco-Spasm Report*. Unfortunately, that book still reads fresh today, with all the news of bank failures and layoffs.

But today's crisis is not like any preceding depression. It's not 1933 all over again. It arises from totally different reasons, and if we are to combat it, we need to recognize what's distinctive about it.

What makes this crisis different is that it is *not* a collapse, but a radical reorganization. It's a crisis of restructure. Until we grasp this fact, and begin to map the outlines of tomorrow's economy, how can we hope to deal with our problems? We need new concepts.

We speak about employment, but we don't even know what "work" will mean in a new society. Indeed, neither work nor, for that matter, unemployment, have the same meaning today that they once did.

■ What do you mean by work?

□ I always make a mental distinction between paid work in the exchange economy and unpaid work in the non-exchange economy

—the activity I call "prosuming." Prosuming is what women, or men, for that matter, do when they raise children....It's what men, or women, for that matter, do when they build an addition onto the house.... It's what people do when they grow their own vegetables, sew their own clothes, or volunteer their services at the hospital. They are producing goods and services. They are working. But not for pay. Prosuming is a key factor in the new economy. But for our purposes now let's stick to the issue of *paid* work—which is what most people mean when they speak of a job.

■ And you say this work itself is being transformed?

☐ Unlike many people who write about it, I've spent years doing some of the nastiest factory work around. Blue-collar work. Manual work. Assembly-line work. I've also visited factories around the world. And I've gone into some of today's most advanced factories and offices to study them.

All of that persuades me that our common images of work are obsolete. They go right back to Adam Smith and Marx on division of labor and alienation. More recently, they go back to C. Wright Mills on the nature of the office. The fact is, we still tend to think of work chiefly in terms of Charlie Chaplin's *Modern Times* or René Clair's *A Nous La Liberté*. All these images and critiques were once accurate. But they apply to traditional industrialism—not to the new system that is rapidly evolving today.

We all know how miserable the fractionalized factory work of the traditional manufacturing industry was—and still is.

And this factory-style of work was transferred into the office, too, each person doing a tiny repetitive task, without any sense of its relationship to the whole, without any pride of skill or craft, without any opportunity for discretion or creativity.

But it is precisely these jobs—these forms of dehumanized work—that are drying up.

What continually amazes me is the nostalgia that argues for the preservation of this kind of work—again, usually from people who have never had to do it.

■ You speak as though all that were in the past tense.

□ Of course not. Millions of workers, from assemblers to typists, even in the most technologically advanced nations, are still trapped in miserable jobs requiring that kind of work.

But the key to the future of work is the recognition that routine, repetitive, fragmented work is no longer efficient. It is already outmoded in the high technology nations. So those kinds of jobs will continue to decline, no matter what companies, unions and governments do. We ought not weep and moan about it.

And something is already beginning to take its place. It's part of the restructuring of the economy I spoke of earlier.

The expansion of the Third Wave sector implies a wholly different kind of work.

There already are—or soon will be—new occupations, from PET-scan* technicians in hospitals, to resource recyclers, to speech-recognition unit repair people, to people who set up and coordinate home production, to people who engage in manganese mining of the oceans, to materials designers, to solar photovoltaic panel installers, to under-sea archaeologists and fiber optics line persons, to space lab architects, to direct broadcast satellite programmers, learning theorists, video trainers, and teleconference consultants.

Few, if any, of these new-style occupations lend themselves to the kind of routine, Taylorized labor that characterized most jobs in the past.

■ But we've always had diverse types of jobs. Aren't these examples of technological exotica? What about more ordinary jobs? Can't technological innovations be screened and contoured to preserve sharp hierarchies of labor and fragmentation of work? If we allow it, won't liberating technologies be ignored while technologies that preserve today's hierarchical relationships are rushed into production?

*Positron Emission Tomography scanners provide us with cross-sectional images of energy flows in the brain.

◻ Of course, no one likes to give up power. The lowliest foreman and the highest executive may both have a stake in maintaining old-style work relationships. But the odds are shifting against them. In traditional, Second Wave industries, fragmented, repetitive, mindless work paid off for the company. Today computers can very often do that kind of work faster and better, and robots can do the dangerous work. The old forms of work are less and less profitable and productive. So there is an incentive to change them.

Not long ago I stood in the assembly area of a Silicon Valley computer company. This was not chip manufacture—which is still very largely organized along Second Wave lines, with rows of workers, mostly women, mostly in Asia, doing miserable repetitive factory work. That is still mass manufacture. By contrast, the company I visited takes those chips and makes end-products out of them. And what I saw was a totally different style of work.

It was typical of de-massified production. The physical surroundings were clean and quiet. The assembly room was bright and cheerful, the workbenches cluttered with plants, family photos, and memorabilia. Workers had small radios and sometimes Walkman stereo units.

The work, itself, was the opposite of what one would expect. Instead of performing one small task over and over again, these assemblers each performed many complex operations and tests on a very small number of units each day. There was no mechanical assembly line at all.

I don't want to imply that their work was all fun and games. It wasn't. But the contrast between this and the old-style work was striking, and it is this kind of Third Wave work that is expanding, while the Second Wave sector declines.

In Second Wave industries, you're getting layoffs and wage cuts, deferred benefits, tighter and tighter pressures on the worker.

In Third Wave industries, the talk is all about employee participation in decision-making; about job enlargement and enrichment, instead of fractionalization; about flex-time instead of rigid hours; about cafeteria-style fringe benefits which give employees a choice, rather than a *fait accompli*; about how to encourage creativity rather than blind obedience.

CREATIVE WORK-STYLES

■ But proportionately for each of these assemblers you saw, how many women in Taiwan are working in sweatshop conditions creating parts? And how many workers here in the U.S. are out of work completely? There are only so many slots in a capitalist economy for highly skilled intellectual workers. For everyone to enjoy the conditions you describe would require changes in organization, not just production, and in education and socialization as well. In a sense, the current class structure would be squeezed, most everyone becoming a kind of professional/managerial type within a quite cooperative overall structure. But to achieve this, assuming it is desirable, would require a vast move in the direction of much greater equalization of knowledge and prerogative. Those who now have advantages are likely to resist, aren't they? And aren't the more human conditions you describe in some high tech industries largely a function of the exceptionally high levels of growth and profitability these shops are enjoying?

□ Sure. The fact that the new high tech industries are relatively profitable makes it easier. And the fact that high skills are in short supply gives those who have them bargaining power. All that is true. But it's not enough to explain what's happening. Look at it this way: Work was brutal and miserable in Second Wave industries even when these industries were highly profitable. In fact, the brutality of the work contributed directly to the profits. The harder you sweated people, the more money you made.

In many Third Wave companies, exactly the opposite is true. Brutality in the workplace no longer pays off—it's counter-productive.

Third Wave companies don't increase profits by sweating their employees. They don't succeed by working harder, but by working *smarter*. Sweat just doesn't pay off the way it once did.

To dramatize the difference, we might say that in the old mass production industries, it was muscles that counted. In the advanced, de-massified industries, information and imagination are crucial, and that changes everything.

I remember one of my conversations in Tokyo with Akio Morita, the co-founder of Sony. He put it plainly. "I can tell a factory worker to show up at 7:00 AM sharp and produce. But I can't tell a researcher or engineer to show up at 7:00 and have a creative idea."

Morita knows this, and so do the other successful people in the Third Wave industries. Talk to Steve Jobs of Apple or to Jim Treybig of Tandem Computers.

And when Third Wave companies get into trouble, it's because of a badly designed product, inadequate marketing, poor organization, or other reasons. It isn't because their employees are sweating inadequately.

The character of the work itself is different, and it takes a completely different kind of worker.

THE NEW WORKER

■ In your view, exactly how does the new-style worker differ from the old?

□ The Third Wave worker is more independent, more resourceful, no longer an appendage of the machine. Typically, a worker with skills or specialized knowledge. And like the artisan before the industrial revolution, who owned a kit of hand-tools, the new "mind-workers," if you want to call them that, have skills and information that amount to a kit of head-tools. They own the "means of production," in a way that unskilled factory workers never could.

The new workers are more like independent craft workers than interchangeable assembly line hands. They are younger, better educated. They absolutely detest routine. They want to be left alone by the boss to get the job done their own way. They want a say. They are used to change, ambiguity, flexible organization. They represent a new force and their numbers are multiplying.

As the economy shifts from Second Wave to Third Wave, we're getting a new set of values along with the new skills, and that has deep implications for employers, for government policy, for Marxist economics, for trade unions....

■ We can agree that this type of "mind-work" exists in society and makes for a better work situation. No doubt such workers have a degree of self-confidence, and demand—even sometimes get— some flexibility and sense of participation. But how many do?

And what factors determine how far the trend toward this type of work-style will go?

You point to changes in technology and the importance of knowledge in production as critical factors. But what about the desire of existing social groups to maintain their relative advantages. Won't capitalists oppose the incursion on their status and power that will inevitably accompany growing autonomy and say for intellectual workers? Won't current professionals and managers jealously guard their relative monopoly on intellectual work and the "superior position" it gives them vis-à-vis other workers? Even now, doesn't the AMA try to limit the number of doctors? And don't managers in companies like IBM oppose excessive moves toward worker participation?

In the new industries you envision, how changed is the basic structure? Are employees still employees, expected to make a profit for the firm, no matter the personal or social cost?

In short, are you envisioning a new workplace where everyone shares the rote tasks and is equally a self-managing partner in the whole industrial project? Or do you really see just a slightly altered version of what we have: more intellectual workers, to be sure, but still bosses with ultimate power and plenty of traditional workers to carry out rote tasks?

□ I'm not a utopian. And I don't imagine a perfect workplace emerging in which everyone shares equally in decisional authority, rote work, and economic reward. Nor would I regard that as perfect, even if achievable. Such a system might work well under some circumstances; it might be a catastrophe under others. Some people might enjoy working in such an enterprise—others might hate it.

A good society should offer maximum variety—jobs that are structured for you and jobs you structure yourself; jobs that demand participation and others that don't. Most utopians and socialists, in my experience, still think in terms of Second Wave uniformity.

If what I'm saying about de-massification of society is correct, we are likely to see an explosion of new organizational forms of the most diverse kinds. Instead of economies made up of private enterprises or state enterprises, or even a mixture of these, we may well find "electronic co-ops," religious and familial production teams, non-profit work networks—more arrangements than we can now imagine.

Among these, no doubt, will be self-managing enterprises, as well. Above a certain size, self-managed enterprises have never been a great success until now, so far as I am aware. But one of the overlooked things about "mind-workers" is that they are far better equipped to manage themselves than typical workers of the past. So various new forms of self-management may proliferate.

For the near term, however, depending upon the country, we are still basically talking about either state-run or private companies. They will come under increasing pressure to reorganize along less bureaucratic, less hierarchical lines. The more the economy and society move into the Third Wave, the less efficient these traditional forms of organization become.

And as for pursuit of the bottom line—of course, firms will pursue profit, but not only profit. Smart companies no longer attempt to maximize profit, no matter what Milton Friedman tells them, but that is a separate matter. Let's come back to it later. For the moment, let's stick with work, because what I'm saying about its changed character has powerful political implications.

As the nature of work changes, you can almost see the emergence of two distinct working classes—if that term still applies.

We have always had divisions in the working class, of course. But the ideal of the trade unions and of the left and radical movements always revolved around notions of solidarity, unity, joint effort, uniformity of treatment, equal pay, identical fringe benefits, etc.

In both capitalist and existing socialist countries, the industrial production system required a standardized, uniform workforce, and it can almost be argued that the trade unions helped create this for the employers. Whether or not that's so, the entire system suppressed diversity and individuality. Marx argued that the factory system itself promoted the collectivization of consciousness, so that all workers would eventually come to see themselves as members of the same class—the "working masses."

What's happening now is the dialectical opposite—it's Marx on his head, if you will. Because in the rising sectors of the economy, you don't need thousands of workers doing uniform, standardized, repetitive work. What the system needs are workers who are resourceful, innovative, educated, even individualistic.

That kind of worker is now at a premium in the advanced sectors of the economy, and he or she is not easy for unions to recruit. These people will invent their own new forms of organization—more associational, less homogenizing. And if they do join unions, they will force important changes in union structure, practice and ideology.

The new work styles, the new values, the new diversity and individualization fit in perfectly with the de-massification of production, consumption, communication, energy, and family structure.

In fact, the changes in all these other spheres help determine what is happening in the economic sphere, so it isn't just the economy driving the rest of the system.

Just as consumers increasingly demand customized goods and services, workers (very often the same consumers wearing a different hat) demand customized treatment on the job. And, whereas in the past, Second Wave technology promoted uniformity, Third Wave technology caters to and actually encourages social diversity.

It's a self-reinforcing reality.

ON REWARDS AND WELFARE

■ Are you suggesting that we are creating an economy in which only people who get a higher education and develop specialized job skills will find work? What good will it be if we succeed in humanizing certain jobs, but then structure education and the economy as a whole to exclude the majority of people from employment in them?

☐ It would be a tragedy if we built an economy around cognitive skills only...if we rewarded only people who were good at abstract reasoning and verbal articulation—a "literocracy."

But I don't see that as likely. A Third Wave economy, even if it has a heavy information base, requires all sorts of human talents and resources—not just sheer unalloyed brainpower. And I believe the economy will provide incentives for other kinds of skills as well. For example, we will need large numbers of trainers and retrainers. That requires interpersonal skills, or visual, graphic and dramatic skills. We're going to need people who are good at empathy, people who have aesthetic and athletic skills, people who are sensitive managers and organizers—and that requires a lot more than cognitive ability. We need fighters and conciliators and cross-cultural communicators and many other types of human beings.

The idea that any society, or even the paid economy, can be run on disembodied I.Q. is a myth. It's propagated by technocrats, but it simply isn't true.

The question is how to reward the great variety of skills needed.

No civilization has ever rewarded all skills equally—nor should it. Agricultural or First Wave civilization paid off for certain traits and skills, especially raw muscle power. Industrial or Second Wave civilization paid off for different skills. Third Wave civilization will also reward some traits and skills better than others.

In each period, those with poorly rewarded skills had to accept a lesser role in society or had to fight to change the reward system. I suspect the same will be true in the future.

And that takes me back to the idea of some form of guaranteed minimum income for all who make a contribution to production. Whether this is done through a negative income tax, as I think was proposed by Milton Friedman, or along lines set out by economists like Robert Theobald, I think that all the high technology societies will have to move in this direction. Such systems need not be centralized or standardized. They might even flow through the private sector. We can be highly creative as to method. But unless the high tech countries deal with this issue, they will face explosive social conflicts.

■ But aren't today's attacks on the welfare society taking us in precisely the opposite direction?

□ I didn't say anything about *welfare*. I said we would need to reward all who make a contribution to production. That's different. It's not the same as a welfare system, and it's not the same as rewarding only those with jobs. It's something inherently different from both.

What I'm talking about doesn't fit any of the old categories, right or left, liberal or conservative.

I am *not* saying we should reward non-producing members of society, as the welfare system sometimes does.

I am saying that there are many people who *do* produce wealth and value for society, but who are invisible to our conventional economists and thinkers. I'm speaking about unrecognized producers.

Many consumers, for example, contribute to production outside the exchange economy, as I pointed out in *The Third Wave*. They produce real goods and services for themselves, relieving society of the need to do so. Millions of women fit in this category. And they contribute value to the exchange economy, itself. Only they do so by working in the *use* economy, so we never notice them. They are what I call "prosumers." In addition, even within the exchange sector, many third parties co-produce value, but are not recognized—like the case of the television station that helped expand farm production.

Prosumers and co-producers are the very opposite of non-productive. But their contributions are invisible because we use archaic, unjust systems of accounting.

I'm not saying give everyone a welfare-handout. I'm saying we must recognize true contributions to productivity and reward them. In fact, I suspect we can't solve the unemployment crisis until we do so.

SEVEN STREAMS OF UNEMPLOYMENT

■ You insist we're moving toward a new form of economy. Yet here we face the oldest of problems—unemployment. Why is it so different from what we have endured in the past? And how should we grapple with it?

□ We could keep everyone working if we were willing to pay the price. War, for example. It's economic amphetamine—but, like the real thing, it can do you in.

We can also create non-jobs and pay people to perform them. The economy is already full of that. The Soviets are masters of full employment through the simple expedient of proliferating bureaucratic non-jobs.

The Western antidote for unemployment, at least since Keynes and Roosevelt, has been growth. But even if we didn't have OPEC and inflation to worry about, growth policies by themselves are unlikely to eliminate high levels of unemployment.

Because the unemployment problem is not simply quantitative. It is no longer simply a question of how many jobs. It's what *kind* of jobs, where, when, and who can fill them. It's a qualitative issue. If you don't face the qualitative issue, you can't solve the quantitative problem.

The economy requires more different skills than ever before, and the skill needs keep changing at an accelerated pace. The work force is more diverse. The economy itself is more differentiated, more frenetic and flux-like. Today's economy is rashy, with pockets of depression next door to booming industries. As a result, we can no longer solve the problem with simple, across-the-board measures.

Unemployment, itself, is more diverse in its origins.

■ For the unemployed mother trying to raise a couple of kids alone or for the 50-year-old laid-off auto worker unemployment probably feels similar, even if it has diverse causes.

☐ Yes, but you can't cure the disease with a single medicine. You're actually dealing with more than half a dozen identifiably different diseases. Lumping them all together under the heading "unemployment" is like calling cancer a single disease. And most of our remedies for unemployment are potentially deadly—they're like whole-body radiation.

The fact is I can rattle off at least seven distinctly different streams that feed overall unemployment.

First, there's the *structural* unemployment that arises out of the shift from Second Wave to Third Wave industries. This is happening on a world scale. As old, traditional industries collapse, or relocate in places like Thailand or Mexico, they leave gaping holes in the industrialized economies and millions are left jobless.

One result of this upheaval is an intensification of international trade pressures, rivalries, dumping, imbalances, sudden lurches and upsets in the world market. This creates a second stream of joblessness —*trade-related* unemployment.

There's an additional generalized pressure on jobs as the levels of technology improve and fewer and fewer workers are needed to turn out a given level of production. This is the familiar, controversial, *technological* unemployment.

There is unemployment that results from purely local and regional causes—local overproduction, shifts in consumer preferences, mergers, ecological problems, etc.—let's call this *"normal"* unemployment.

There's also a higher than usual level of *frictional* unemployment—the unavoidable, essentially temporary joblessness of people who are in the process of shifting from one job to another. The faster things move, the more accelerated change becomes, the higher this total is likely to be. And rates of change today are very high.

There's also unemployment that is almost wholly a result of the breakdown of information. As the division of labor becomes even more refined, there are fewer and fewer interchangeable jobs. The problem of matching the skill to the task, which was relatively easy when most workers did routine, interchangeable jobs, becomes far more difficult. This calls for a far more sophisticated information system than now exists. Until it's created, we can expect serious levels of *informational* unemployment.

Finally, there is what I call *iatrogenic* unemployment—the unintended unemployment that flows from stupid government policies—often policies intended to increase employment.

I suspect that a very significant proportion of our non-structural unemployment is of this character. It is disease caused by the doctor, and it can kill you. Unfortunately, politicians and economists aren't liable for malpractice suits.

We could list many more streams of unemployment, all of them criss-crossing and overlapping. I've done this only to make the point that it isn't a single problem. There are many interwoven problems, and the complexity is enormous.

Bear in mind, for example, that when we say that technology can cause unemployment, we're only looking at one of its effects. It can also create jobs elsewhere in the system, and usually does.

Indeed, even unemployment increases employment. It makes jobs for social workers, doctors and police. It alters wage levels in certain industries and may create new employment opportunities at lower wage levels.

Everything we do has multiple consequences, each of which, in turn, has second order, third order, and nth order consequences of its own. As the system de-massifies and grows more complex, our existing models lose whatever power they may once have had.

In any case, the notion that "unemployment" is a single aggregate problem, that it is quantitative, as distinct from qualitative, is a typical, obsolete industrial idea. It is based on the assumption that we're still dealing with a traditional mass economy.

Like the economy itself, unemployment is increasingly differentiated in terms of its causes—and hence its cures. Each of these types of unemployment has to be attacked in its own terms. We are still trying to treat the illness with broadband antibiotics, rather than "smart," closely targeted medicines.

■ And which of these streams of unemployment do you see as most important?

□ Overall, the joblessness that arises from the decay of Second Wave industries and the rise of new ones based on new skills and cultural attitudes. Structural unemployment.

In the classical recession or depression, the factories and offices shut down, and people starved until the same old factories and offices, with the same old jobs, opened up. Today, in many cases, the old factories and offices will not open up ever again, and, when and if they do, chances are they will no longer have the same kinds of jobs. That's why the old remedies won't work. Not monetarist remedies. Not Keynesian remedies. Not Friedman and not Galbraith. Nor will any simple programs based on ideological purity, free enterprise, nationalization, worker control, whatever.

RE-TOOLING THE MIND

■ Realistically, then, will we *ever* be able to put today's structurally unemployed back to work? Steel workers...textile workers...auto workers... not to mention the millions who have never had jobs in the first place?

□ To be hard-nosed, we have to face the fact that many of these laid-off workers will not be reabsorbed into their old jobs—or any jobs in the Second Wave sector of the economy—and that most of these workers are unequipped for the new jobs opening up in the Third Wave sector.

This means one of two things: retirement or retraining.

Unemployment is, in effect, forced retirement. But no modern society can afford large numbers of laid-off workers thrown onto their own meager resources. Mass unemployment without some form of subsidy or benefits will create dangerous political instability and everyone knows it. So the real question is how to pay for the retirement of large numbers of workers from the labor force.

We could force companies to support their own surplus workers through reducing profits. But the industries doing the most laying off are precisely the ones with the lowest profits, and, indeed, some are virtually bankrupt already. So if we compel them permanently to support their own excess labor, they will simply have to pass the costs on to the consumer in the form of increased prices.

Alternatively, we can socialize the costs by making government pay them. In which case the cost is eventually passed along to the public again, this time in the form of taxes. Either way, the costs are spread across much of the public, and these costs could turn out to be enormous.

That's why the other option—retraining—will need to be used wherever possible. I believe, in fact, that we are about to go into the training and retraining business on a tremendous scale. All the high tech societies will have to pour resources into this activity, whether the task is done by the private sector, the education system, the military, the media, or all the above.

This realization is just dawning on the powers that be. We've just had a report submitted to the U.S. Congress that argues the lack of a strategy for retraining "is a major barrier to America's economic renewal." I've had the opportunity to discuss precisely this with top White House officials, and even under an administration committed to free market policies, the recognition is growing that something must be done.

The problem is that when I speak of training or retraining for jobs in the Third Wave industries, I'm speaking of more than just simple occupational skills. The new industries operate in, or create, a new culture as well—they bring new values; they reward new attitudes and life-styles. So for the unemployed steel worker, say, the jump from the mill to one of the new high tech industries could be extremely difficult. It's a cultural jump as well as merely a change in job skills.

Training, in this sense, is very complicated. We don't know how to do it well. And it is likely to be very expensive.

Yet it will be a lot cheaper than simply throwing these workers onto the slag heap and subsidizing their permanent retirement.

Unless we help those who are being progressively squeezed out—help them enter the new cultures as well as the new economy—we are going to tear society apart.

EUTHANASIA FOR DYING INDUSTRIES?

■ If you are right, and we face a basic restructuring of the economy, what can we do to smooth the transition?

□ Long term, we may have to face up to the fact that not everyone can have a "job"—if by that we mean a formal, paid, productive job in the exchange economy.

Eventually we may need to explore "prosuming," ways in which people can produce for themselves, rather than for sale or barter. There are ways in which we could radically increase the productivity of prosuming by providing new tools, materials, social and political support for prosumers, along with some form of monetary support. Such policies sound utopian right now. But they will be at the top of the political agenda very soon. In the meantime, there are more conventional things to do. Unfortunately, we are not even doing these.

Take the Carter Administration in the mid-seventies, or the British Labour Party, when it was in power, or the left and liberal parties in any of these countries. They have basically ignored the new Third Wave industries and devoted themselves to shoring up and preserving the old Second Wave economy.

In the U.S. we try to bail out Chrysler. In the U.K. we quasi-nationalize British Leyland. In France, Germany and other Western European countries, we do the same—we try to keep the managers, unions and stockholders of these traditional industries happy. It's stupid economics. It's blind to the restructuring now taking place. And it's a waste of human lives and effort.

At one point in the debate over Leyland, I calculated that the British government wanted to spend a sum equivalent to seven years' full-time pay for every Leyland worker just to keep Leyland in the car business. It seems to me—given that money, along with training, new technologies, and other supports—those workers could have reorganized their lives and communities over a seven year period, so as no longer to be dependent on making cars. Britain could have created new, healthier industries and communities.

■ Essentially you are suggesting that we should consciously administer the obsolescence of dying industries and of conversion to new Third Wave alternatives, as a matter of government policy—rather than letting market forces rule, unfettered—a kind of careful euthanasia for dying industries?

☐ Yes. We need to be extremely selective about even temporary support, but I could see certain exceptions. For example, if the closure of an industry would destroy an entire region, we might well want to give it a five-year phase-out period to buffer the impact. We might want to keep certain companies alive for other reasons—say as a base for rapid expansion in case of national or international emergency. I can't see the U.S., for example, allowing itself to become totally dependent on the world market for steel or heavy vehicles. It would be foolish to do so. So we might want to keep some specific companies or industries running for social or other reasons.

I know most of the arguments against this policy—and they are not all stupid. The free marketeers have a point when they ask whether political decisions are any better than those made for private economic gain. Look at the French-British decision to build the Concorde! Look at Congress pouring billions into synfuels just as the world price of oil drops. Once investment decisions become political, every interest group goes into high gear. Moreover, industrial policy works best when a country has a clear model to follow—as Japan did after World War II. Today the decisions are much harder to make.

Unfortunately, just leaving things to the invisible hand doesn't work, either.

■ That flies directly in the face of the free market, doesn't it?

□ I'm not a pure marketeer. I do believe that the free market (which is never actually free) is a magnificent regulatory system with the great advantage that, at least to a degree, it separates economic from political power. The market is also a way to decentralize a great many economic decisions. I think we can make far more imaginative use of market mechanisms to cope with social problems like unemployment, urban blight, care of the elderly, pollution, etc., than we have till now.

But any system has limits—that's part of the definition of a system. Our attitudes toward market mechanisms should not be theological. The market is not a religion, it's a tool. And no tool does everything.

Faced with today's unemployment, we shouldn't hesitate to use public funds creatively to phase out certain Second Wave industries. The object should not be to keep them going, not to pay off the managers and workers in them, but to set in motion a process of industrial and regional conversion.

The key is conversion, not support. I wouldn't provide a single buck to support a shrinking industry unless, and until, the industry agrees to draw up a plan for conversion from its present technologies and products to significantly new products and new technologies, along with plans for thoroughly retraining its managers and work force.

A recent *Business Week* poll asked whether dying industries should be allowed to "sink or swim." The magazine gleefully reported that most Americans—56 percent—favored the free market, sink-or-swim approach, rather than "bail-out" support. But those aren't the only alternatives. This either/or approach is simplistic. What is needed is neither a blind survival-of-the-fittest policy nor equally blind hand-outs. What is needed is help in conversion.

Conversion isn't a new idea. There were important discussions of how to go about it at the end of World War II when we wanted to convert from a war-time to a peace-time economy in the U.S. More recently, when the employees of Lucas Aerospace in Britain were told they would face layoffs because of military order cut-backs, they drew up their own plans for alternative products that could be manufactured with more or less the same technology and the same work force. As I understand it, they drew up detailed plans for conversion to the production of things like people movers and medical electronic products.

The Lucas approach bogged down in recrimination between a doctrinaire union and an equally doctrinaire company. But it is instructive. It suggests all sorts of possibilities. And it underscores the point that conversion planning, if it is to work, can't just be done by the corporations. What is needed is a strategy jointly drawn up by the industry, its unions, its employees (not the same as its unions), along with representatives of its suppliers and customers, and of the public agencies of the communities in which it operates. "Conversion" is going to have to be a key word in our economic vocabulary in the near future.

■ In a sense you're suggesting that everyone affected should have a say in the process of conversion—not solely the owners and managers but also the workers, consumers, and community residents? Yet today we hear more and more talk about big business and big government getting together to plan industrial policy.

All your work shows an ambiguous attitude toward planning. On the one hand, from *Future Shock* on, you've called for long-range strategic thinking. But you also emphasize decentralization and diversity. Is there a contradiction in your own thinking?

□ I tried to explain at the end of *Future Shock* the difference between industrial-style, centralized, top-down, bureaucratic planning and a more open, democratic, decentralized style I called "anticipatory democracy." As the economic crisis deepens, I sense mounting support for the idea of strategic planning. But I can't say I like the direction toward which we seem to be moving.

What I hear, as I speak with the board members and top managers of our biggest corporations, is more acceptance of the need for planning, and not just limited to corporations. In the U.S., for example, there is increasing discussion of the Japanese or the West German or the French models of planning. (I find this ironic, since these countries are also in deep difficulty, and it seems to me that much of what passes for "advanced thinking" amounts to no more than swapping obsolete models.) Nevertheless, today the American press is filled with statements by financiers, economists, radical theorists, and multinational corporate executives proclaiming the virtues of "business/government cooperation." Sometimes, the more open-minded and worldly managers say that labor unions also ought to be invited to be part of the planning process.

These themes will no doubt gain support in Washington, irrespective of what administration is in power. The big companies want it. The government wants it, whether it says so or not. And the unions, a poor third when it comes to clout, will also want to be brought to the table.

And though this might be a limited advance over the idiocies that prevail today, it is also frightening to me because it is a kind of internal "trilateralism." It is, in fact, old-style "corporatism" of the kind that fascists toyed with in the twenties.

There are a lot of things wrong—and dangerous—with this model.

First, I don't think it is workable at a national scale in the kind of complex, de-massified economy we are constructing.

Second, it makes the arrogant assumption that if you get companies and unions (which, in the U.S., represent less than a quarter of the work force, often quite undemocratically) and governments together, everyone is "represented." In fact, nobody feels "represented" any longer, least of all by these gigantic institutions.

But the third problem is even deeper. It is that when you get this kind of internal trilateralism going, it becomes an extremely conservative force. It tends to demand support for the *status quo*, for whatever exists. Companies in a weak widget industry want to stay in the widget business. The unions want their jobs and membership dues, so they want the industry to go on making widgets, even when the world no longer wants widgets. And the government isn't going to pick a fight with the other two, if it can be avoided. So the widget plant continues indefinitely and becomes a drag on the economy.

That's why, if there is to be any planning, it must be broken down into smaller pieces, with many more groups brought into the process, everyone from consumers, suppliers, and public agencies, down, perhaps to racial, ethnic, sexual, professional, and other kinds of community groups, with the basic planning done on the local, sectoral, and regional scale, rather than at the national level. It needs to be long-range, not merely short-range, and it needs to take all sorts of non-economic factors into account, like ecology and quality of work.

But having said all this, it is only honest to admit that no one knows how to do this very well without drowning us in paper. There have been many local experiments. Some are promising. The new communications tools, like interactive cable, suggest imaginative new options. But we have not solved the problem of how to define, and continually redefine, relevant constituencies, how to legitimate them, how to tie this entire procedure into the budget and taxation process (without which it remains notional). In short, we have to *invent* the methods and institutions for a truly anticipatory democracy.

I can't pretend to have all the answers, and, yes, there are contradictions. However, one thing is plain to me. We can't go backward. Even if it means a powerful fight against Second Wave industries and trade unions, we need to put our primary emphasis on developing the Third Wave sector. I think we will need to use selective tax credits and a variety of other tools to help accelerate the expansion of the new industries. We ought to encourage more

R&D. Insure loans to small businesses in these fields. Put microcomputers with instructors in every classroom—and in storefronts in every ghetto*. Radically overhaul the education system, and retain, rather than loosen, environmental controls— these indirectly benefit the advanced, Third Wave industries and hasten the transition, because the new industries, with exceptions, tend to be cleaner and more energy-conserving than the old ones.

Surviving this crisis is going to take everything we've got. In addition to these steps plus massive retraining, we may also need subsidies—direct or channeled through the private sector—for a radically expanded service sector. Not merely things like environmental clean-up, but basic human services. Care of the elderly, for example, is going to become a hot political priority as the population ages, not merely in the U.S., but in other countries too, like Japan. This, in fact, opens an opportunity. Because while many of the people laid off in the mass manufacturing sector may not retrain easily for the Third Wave industries, many of them might do very well in Third Wave service occupations. On top of that we'll need imaginative approaches to community development—how to help a community, a mill town, let us say, make the transition to a service center or high tech economy.

I, personally, strongly favor using the private sector as much as possible in carrying through these missions. But, whether private or public, these things will have to be accomplished unless we want to see widespread desperation, not to mention, violence.

There are many steps that might be taken to smooth our transit to a Third Wave economy. We'd better start now.

---

*Two bills have been introduced in the U.S. Congress which move in this direction. One, pushed by Apple Computer, would grant a special tax concession to computer companies that contribute small computers to schools. Another, sponsored by Cong. Newt Gingrich (R-Ga.), would give families the equivalent of a tax investment credit if they purchase a home computer for work or educational purposes.

ROBOTS TO THE RESCUE?

■ You speak of phasing out the old industries. But can't they transform themselves with new technology? Isn't that what some of the big companies are trying to do?

□ Robotizing their plants for example? Yes, of course, smart innovative companies may be able to bootstrap themselves into the new economy, and I know many, many companies that are trying to do this right now. But it takes a lot more than robots.

There are no simple technological fixes because the problem of obsolescence is not simply technological.

In principle, Second Wave enterprises can transform themselves into viable Third Wave enterprises by reducing their dependence on manual labor and employing more brainpower. That's what robotization and automation are all about. Just as we used to substitute energy for manual labor, we are now beginning to substitute information (in its broadest sense) for both.

But to transform successfully, companies or industries have to do a lot of other things as well. They have to restructure themselves organizationally. They have to learn to treat their employees as individuals. They have to customize their products and distribution. They have to contract out more. They have to re-evaluate vertical integration—increasingly, it's a losing strategy. They have to move to smaller units, to more employee participation. There are a whole lot of things that will be needed for survival, not just robots.

■ And what about the workers left behind by all this—the ones replaced by the robots, the ones who aren't immediately prepared to fit into this new society you describe?

□ It seems to me the moral principle is clear. You're a big company and you're in trouble? As management, why didn't you foresee the trouble and head it off in time? That's what you're paid for.

Why did you wait for small foreign cars to take away your market? (Even if big cars were more profitable in the short term, even if gas prices were low, the handwriting was on the wall for years.) Why did you let your furnaces deteriorate, your technological lead slip? Or forget to introduce new products and services? It isn't your workers who are to blame for your troubles today.

So you have a responsibility to them. A 50-year old textile- or auto worker with 18 years in the company has put a lot of sweat equity" into the enterprise. You just don't lay someone like that off. If the company is going to re-tool, it has a responsibility to help its people re-tool also.

■ That's fine ethics, but what about the economics of the situation? The worse off the company is, the less likely it is to help its employees—even if it wanted to.

□ If a company has no resources for this purpose, it is functionally bankrupt and ought to be treated as such. The long-term employee's claim to re-training ought to be treated as the legal equivalent of a supplier's claim for payment of a debt. It's like unpaid wages. And if a company can't pay, then it may need public funds or support. Sometimes that support need not even cost the government anything. Loan guarantees, insurance and other mechanisms are available. But whatever support is given by the government ought not be a hand-out. It should be contingent on the execution of a conversion plan, and if the top executives fail to carry that out, they ought to be held personally responsible. I find it repulsive that the president of a failing company demands wage cuts from the union, in order to salvage the company, but increases his own salary when he is already earning over $400,000 a year. I have no objection, in principle, to executives getting rich, even filthy rich. But they ought to be rewarded for success, not failure.

Our whole notion of investment and renovation will have to be changed for a Third Wave economy. For every dollar we put into new machines, several dollars will have to be invested in human capital—in training, education, relocation, social rehabilitation, in cultural adaptation. Any investment in hardware needs to carry an investment in software along with it.

How much of that cost is externalized by companies, how much absorbed by the public, will vary from country to country, and will no doubt be resolved through hard-ball politics and economic struggle.

But the core of the matter remains: conversion in industry after industry. Wherever possible, the conversion of people, not just machines.

■ You attack the "bail-out" approach to dying industries...

☐ Without some strategy for conversion, it's nostalgia. It's futile and wasteful.

■ What about the free market approach?

☐ I've already said, that's even worse. It lacks even the charm of good intentions.

It's based on a complete misreading of the new economy. It assumes that as the older industries die and lay workers off, new ones will crop up and absorb the surplus.

The assumption is that the economic machine can be manipulated to keep unemployment at the right level to keep wage demands down at least to the level of productivity increase, without at the same time generating the kind of social turmoil that would threaten the country.

The assumption is that some mixture of correct monetary, tax or spending policies will produce this condition, spurring the economy just enough so that most of the unemployed can go back to their old jobs or into the newer industries. But that won't happen. Many of the old jobs are gone for good. And it's naive to assume that somehow all those millions of laid-off textile workers, foundry workers, auto workers, steel workers, rubber workers, and apparel workers will find jobs in the computer industry, or in communications, or genetics, or elsewhere in the Third Wave economy.

Laissez-faire is at least as idiotic as blind bail-outs for the old sector. Both are inherently nostalgic.

The laissez-faire approach presupposes that workers are interchangeable. It assumes that the kinds of skills needed in the Third Wave sector are the same as those in the Second Wave sector and that the same type of workers, with the same attitudes, lifestyles, and values are needed in both. Its image of the labor force is obsolete.

The invisible hand needs help. To work—for the Third Wave sector to sop up unemployment in the Second Wave sector— something has to happen. Even assuming no net loss in numbers of jobs, those millions of people have to be retrained and adapted before they can be useful in the new industries. To assume that that process of re-tooling will occur by itself, magically, without added support for education, training and other efforts, is to believe in the tooth fairy.

■ But will a government dominated by big business ever agree to such policies? In the light of political trends in the U.S. and other countries, isn't what you propose likely only if popular movements fight for it?

□ The issue isn't big business. Yes, of course, political struggle is needed. But the issue is Second Wave vested interests (including corporate, government, and labor union interests) vs. Third Wave forces (which include some corporations, some union members,* some public groups—consumer, environmentalist, regionalist, etc.). There is the basis for what might be called a "Third Wave coalition" around the idea of human and industrial conversion and

---

*Most trade unions are firmly anchored in the past and even reject the idea of long-range planning. In the U.S. Lane Kirkland, President of the AFL-CIO, sneers at the idea of looking ahead to the year 2000. By contrast, the Communications Workers of America, most of whose 650,000 members work in the U.S. telephone system, has established its own Committee on the Future to help prepare it for a role in the "information age." Its primary goal: more retraining for members in order that they may be able to use the advanced communication technologies of tomorrow. Some unions are at least potential allies in the advance toward a Third Wave economy. But even when unions are not, many of their members are.

renewal. Certainly, the one issue we ought to be able to mobilize considerable support for is education/training.

And that takes us back to what I was saying before.

What is needed is a massive effort to redeploy labor through training, retraining, and still more training. Training is going to be one of the biggest Third Wave industries of all. It will even become a significant export industry.

And again, when I say training, I don't just mean for specific mechanical job skills, like key-punching. I mean something we don't know how to do very well: helping people transition to wholly new ways of life.

Whether we call that training or education or something else doesn't much matter. What matters is that this kind of transition support is necessary if we aren't going to tear the society apart.

Even if we knew how to do it, I don't believe it can be done just by the private sector, though we ought to try a thousand different approaches and we ought to heavily subsidize private sector training through tax and other measures. We also need to radically re-think our education system.

Even with such efforts, there is still going to be a great deal of disruption and social turmoil.

THE JOB AS ANACHRONISM

■ We've covered a lot of territory. Can you sum up the key points, then, in the form of policy recomendations?

☐ 1. The concept of a "job" is an anachronism, a product of the industrial revolution. As the industrial age ends, the concept will either eventually fade away, or it must be realistically redefined to include many activities that are productive—but unpaid. Re-think the meaning of terms like "job," "employment," "unemployment."

2. Start preparing conversion plans now for all the threatened Second Wave industries. The "basic" industries, as we've known them, will never be basic again.

3. Nurture the new basic industries: telecommunications, biotechnology, ocean engineering, software, information, electronics, etc.

4. Invent and expand services—another new basic and a key to future employment. Focus on human problems: the elderly, health, loneliness, childcare. (This sector can be transformed from a bastion of governmental bureaucracy to a decentralized entrepreneurial sector based on small units serving micro-markets and consisting of small businesses, non-profits, co-ops, plus public agencies.)

5. Training yet again. In fact, training itself can be a big employer as well as a gigantic customer for video equipment, computers, games, films and other products which also provide jobs.

6. Break up the mass education system. Today's schools are turning out still more factory-style workers for jobs that won't exist. Diversify. Individualize. Decentralize. Smaller, more local schools. More education in the home. More parental involvement. More creativity, less rote (it's the rote jobs that are disappearing the fastest).

7. Even with all this, large numbers will not find new jobs. But they can be productive, if we help them produce needed, valuable goods and services *outside* the job market. That means designing new products, materials, tools, even new crops that they can produce for themselves, given some instruction and support services. The "prosumer" or self-help sector can take a load off the exchange sector, while still making possible a decent life for millions.

8. Finally, minimum income guarantees. (Even prosumers need some money income.) Such transfer payments don't have to come through the conventional channels. They can be handled as negative income taxes, or they can be decentralized, privatized, funnelled through families, churches, schools, businesses, local governments and a thousand other pipelines, so as to reduce the centralized bureaucracy and the accumulation of power in the hands of Big Brother.

Only by putting these and more conventional policies together into a coherent package will we begin to dent the unemployment crisis. Once we explode the old, narrow conception of production and recognize that millions contribute to making it possible—even if they, themselves, hold no formal job—we lay the moral basis for a totally new, humane system of rewards that match the fresh options opened for us by a Third Wave economy.

3 THE JAPANESE (AND OTHER) MYTHS

When I was a child I had toys that were made in Japan. Tiny paper umbrellas, miniature trucks and cars, harmonicas...Toys were a major Japanese export, and they were known throughout the West as examples of the shoddiest, most imitative of mass manufactured products.

Today the tide of Western opinion has swung so far in the other direction that Japanese products are universally admired for their quality. The press has suddenly begun to picture Japan as a superstate whose executives possess near-magical skills. Japan, proclaims the title of an influential book, is "Number One."

My wife, Heidi, and I have made many trips to Japan. We have met with Prime Ministers, professors, top executives, union officials, planners, economists, architects, and authors. The more frequently we visit Japan, the more we realize how little we know about the complexity of this ancient culture. One thing I do know, however: just as racist and patronizing attitudes of the West toward Japan blinded us in the past, so, once more, we are basing important decisions on a simplistic misreading of that complex country.

We are victims of the myth of Japanese invincibility.

—A.T.

■ We're going to focus here on the new role of Japan, and also on the efforts being made by other nations to come to terms with the decline of industrial society. But let's start with your own experience. When did you first visit Japan?

□ In April, 1970, shortly before *Future Shock* was published, I went to Kyoto for the International Future Research Congress. Since then, and especially in recent years, Heidi and I have gone back and forth with some frequency—often on lecture tours, or to attend a scholarly conference, sometimes in connection with my books, lately because of our television co-production with the Japan Broadcasting Corp. (NHK).

■ You mentioned earlier that the television program involved a multicultural effort with Canadian, American, and Japanese crews. Was the Japanese version the same as the Western version?

□ No. While we shot much material in common, Japanese television styles are different. So the editing and presentation differed. The response in Japan was awesome. When the Japanese first aired it on prime time on a Friday night, they expected an audience of 7,000,000. They actually reached an audience of 12,000,000. The program went on to win one of Japan's top television awards.

■ You had appeared on Japanese television before, hadn't you?

□ Yes, I gave a series of lectures to the country's top leadership in the winter of 1980. One of these was broadcast nationwide on prime time—70 uninterrupted minutes, in effect an address to the Japanese nation.

■ What was the gist of the message?

□ That Japan's stunning economic successes in the 60s and 70s meant that Japan had learned how to play the game of industrialization. But that a new era was approaching, and that just because Japan knows how to make cheap, high quality cars, steel or TV sets doesn't mean it will necessarily do well in the restructured economy of the future.

■ One of the things we, in the West, hear frequently is that Japan is more productive than we are. How do you react to that?

☐ It is a misperception. Heidi and I have, in fact, written about that. The first problem is the definition of productivity. It is one of the spongiest, most treacherous of economic concepts. It was designed for a world of material production, when you could count how many workers and how many hours it took to turn out how many skirts or copper bars.

As we have moved toward what I've been calling a Third Wave economy, more and more of our output consists of information, services, experiences. More and more, the consumer's own actions affect the efficiency of the producer. In addition, we have begun to appreciate that economic "productivity" is frequently more an artifact of accounting and of permissible externalizations than of anything else. So I have tremendous problems with the very term "productivity."

But even if we use the old, anachronistic definitions, the idea that Japan is more productive is false.

You have to understand that the West's image of Japan is a naive hodge-podge of stereotypes. First we looked upon it as an exotic little country—*Madame Butterfly* and *The Mikado* writ large. Then we looked upon it as the bloodthirsty imperialist power that attacked us without reason. After the war, we looked on Japan patronizingly as America's junior partner—backward little yellow people eager to learn from the West. Now we look at it as an invincible competitor incapable of innovation, and hence reduced to stealing our technological secrets. This harks back to the old racist stereotype of the "sneaky Oriental" once more. All these are absurd comic book images, yet some of our most intelligent Western businessmen and government leaders, not to mention millions of ordinary people, believe them.

Respected academics soberly discuss whether or not Japan is "Number One"—as though nations or cultures could be ranked like baseball teams.

■ But is Japan more productive?

□ Certain industries surely are—a few big export industries. These are the ones other nations have to compete against, so everyone is aware of them. We see millions of Toyotas and Panasonics and are astonished at how fast and inexpensively they are made.

But that's a very biased sample. When you look at many other industries, you find that, even by the old measures, Japan is behind the U.S. and the Common Market countries in productivity. On top of that, their distribution system is frequently criticized for being unproductive. All you have to do is count the number of clerks behind the counter in stores like Mitsukoshi or Hankyu in the Ginza to wonder what they are all doing there. In addition, Japan is a nation of mom-and-pop stores, tiny, labor-intensive, etc. And the same goes for its agriculture. So even if we apply the conventional criteria, the notion that Japan is economically more productive is certainly open to challenge. What's interesting is the reverse of this. One could argue that Japan is more socially productive, in many ways.

THE MOM-AND-POP CULTURE

■ What do you mean by social productivity?

□ Take the two sectors I've mentioned—retail and agriculture. While a conventional economist might say it is inefficient to have tiny, labor-intensive farms which are indirectly subsidized by the government, it is clear that the preservation of this sector maintains a degree of social stability. It provides many Japanese with a way of life which is half in the industrial economy, half out. It permits many to work part time in the factory, part time in the fields.

Similarly, the hundreds of thousands of tiny mom-and-pop stores represent not merely an economic structure, but a certain kind of family life and culture: the shopkeeper class, with its particularly strong family ties. One might call that socially valuable.

The Liberal-Democratic Party (conservative by U.S. or European standards) draws a lot of support from these sectors and, in turn, protects them with direct or indirect subsidies.

Once you look beneath the surface, you find out that the fabled productivity often vanishes in a puff of smoke. It's high in export, low elsewhere. It's high in exported autos or steel, but low in domestic utilities and other services. By contrast with the U.S., it's low in aluminum, pharmaceuticals, chemicals, food and other industries. It's high in large-scale mass manufacturing which is shrinking—but low in the white collar sector, which is rapidly expanding. In fact, the Japanese office is a paragon of low productivity. It's almost Dickensian, with thousands of male clerks working with helter-skelter files in crowded, disorganized layouts, and hordes of young girls who open doors, run errands, and serve tea to visitors.*

According to Prof. Kazukiyo Kurosawa of the Tokyo Institute of Technology, who specializes in the study of white collar

---

*Part of the backwardness of the white collar sector in Japan can be traced to the Japanese language, itself. Because English and other alphabetic languages use a small number of characters, they are easily reducible to a typewriter keyboard and a filing system. With these technologies, the West standardized office work, just as it standardized factory work after the industrial revolution. By contrast, Japanese uses thousands of Chinese ideographic characters along with many Japanese phonetic signs, and much office work still relies on hand-work. In effect, the Japanese office is still operated in a First Wave mode. The recent invention of Japanese word-processors, however, could lead to a major breakthrough. Like some "developing countries," the Japanese office may be able to "skip a stage" and move directly from First Wave to Third Wave.

productivity, American offices are 30-50 per cent more productive than their Japanese counterparts. Jon Woronoff, whose books on Japan clear away a lot of the academic smoke, deals with this in his book *Japan's Wasted Workers.*

We also tend to forget that Japan is experiencing the same wrenching dislocations as the West in restructuring its economy. It is pouring resources into Third Wave sectors like computers, chips and biotechnology. But simultaneously it is suffering hard times in its Second Wave sectors. For all the competition they give the West, Japan's steel producers are operating at 66 per cent of capacity. Textiles are in trouble. So are most of the traditional industries.

■ Do you regard the life-time employment system as another example of social efficiency?

□ Westerners seem to have the idea that Japanese workers are never fired—that, once hired the worker is retained by the company forever. And it is often said that this system is a vestige of feudalism. The notion is wrong on both counts.

To begin with, the life-time employment system cannot be traced directly back to feudalism. It actually was introduced at various times in the 1930s and 1950s, depending upon the industry.

Next, it does not apply to all workers or all industries. Many small enterprises do not offer guaranteed employment. Even in the larger companies, the system doesn't apply to all. Women, for example, are frequently classed as temporary or provisional workers and therefore not counted. So are many young men. (It is hard to know exactly what percentage of workers are included since very often the system is informal and not part of the employment contract.) McKinsey, the consulting firm, recently estimated that only 35 per cent of Japanese workers are actually protected.

And the length of the guaranteed "life-time" is itself shrinking. I remember a Japanese joke about high rents and the fact that the yen buys less and less space each year. The Japanese do not measure floorspace in feet or meters, but in a unit based on the size of an ordinary tatami mat. A room might be six tatamis or ten tatamis. And as room size shrank, the joke was that "the tatami was getting smaller." The same is happening to the length of a "lifetime." Employees—including top executives—are nudged, sometimes booted, into earlier and earlier retirement, or they are rehired at a fraction of their regular pay.

In fact, the system, which worked well in periods of rapid expansion, is now in danger of coming apart. It remains to be seen how long Japanese companies can live up to the life-long commitment in periods of sharp contraction.

Nonetheless, for as long as it lasts, the system does buffer many people against the ups and downs of the economy. It's an important stabilizer, for those who have it, and it accelerates technical change in Japan.

■ How is that?

□ Because, to the degree that workers are protected, they do not fear and resist the latest technologies—they frequently welcome computers, robots and other innovations. One could argue that this is a form of social productivity that then pays off in economic productivity.

But this does not mean, as some people believe, that Japan will race into the future faster than any other nation. No country is "Number One." The very notion is uni-dimensional. Every nation has its own advantages and disadvantages as the entire industrial civilization is transformed.

NOSTALGIA—THE ENGLISH DISEASE

■ How would you compare the U.S., Japan, and Europe in these respects?

□ Japan has several powerful advantages in addition to the one I just mentioned—its embrace of computer technology, its willingness to accept high technology. Over and above this, it has a degree of future-consciousness that is astonishing. The British—also an island people—are forever wallowing in the past, mourning their lost empire, engaging in jingo theatrics, putting on magnificent television programs about the Age of Elizabeth or the Victorian era, and filling their bookstores and magazines with nostalgia. The Japanese like nothing better than to think, talk, debate, imagine, quarrel about and stimulate each other with images of the future. This doesn't mean they have lost their past. I dare say the past is far more present in Japan, even today, than in Britain. But the public is more attuned to the future and to change. The key to this, I think, is their collective sense of insecurity—even paranoia.

The British have displayed the reverse—numb complacency in the face of looming disaster. The Japanese, by contrast, tend to be great worriers. I think a great deal has to do with Britain's colonial successes in the past, which give the present generation of British leaders an inflated sense of Britain's power and significance. By contrast, the Japanese are keenly aware that their imperial adventures brought them nothing but incredible pain and destruction. I think that keen awareness is a key to Japan's survival.

Britain is not only saddled with cultural attitudes that make *any* change painful, her technological base is decrepit, and political power is shared by two parties that are virtually locked into Second Wave industry. The lack of proportional representation and the internal rigging of the parties and the election system centralize great power in the parties, which are in turn dependencies of the great unions, on the one side, and the big employers, on the other.

The Labour Party almost seems to hanker for a return to the 1930s, when the lines were all clear, and parts of it are coming under the control of a doctrinaire Trotskyite faction whose vision goes back to 1917. The Tories, given their choice, seem to prefer a return to the even better days of 1830.

Trapped in between you have the Liberals and the small Social Democratic Party built around people like David Owen and Shirley Williams, who are inherently more open, constructive, and nondoctrinaire—but whose programs reflect a search for the obsolete middle, rather than any solid understanding of the emerging new society.

As a result, the resistance to innovation in Britain tends to be fierce. British operations researchers laid the base, during World War II, for many of today's advances in information and communication. But British business failed to capitalize on these innovations by creating new, Third Wave industries based on them. British engineers and scientists in recent years have led in the transmission of data by telephone and over-the-air to user TV screens, and there is now even an experimental pay-TV system in Milton Keynes based on fiber optic technology.

But when the government, after dawdling, finally announced it would permit cable television, the response from the old power barons was instantaneous and savage. The British Broadcasting Corporation charged that cable television would fragment the nation (meaning the BBC audience); and the trade unions swung into attack on the spurious grounds that cable would reduce employment (when, in fact, the reverse is more likely).

Any move seen to weaken the dominance of the old centralist elites, in coal, steel, auto, broadcasting or any other field, is immediately ridiculed and resisted. It is almost as though England, having given birth to the industrial age, now resents any effort to leave it behind. Until Britain cracks the two-party hammerlock on its political system, its outlook remains grim.

THE FRENCH DISCONNECTION

■ And the rest of Europe?

□ France is inching forward by fits and starts. Like Japan it is over-centralized. The Mitterrand government talked about decentralizing government and decentralizing Paris. But when it came to economic power, it moved toward further centralization.

On the other hand, quite unlike the British, the French have shown a keen interest in what they call "informatique"—telecommunications and computing—which is critical to their future. Here again, the recent government appears to swing back and forth between announcing grandiose decentralist plans and then cutting back in actuality. France talked about democratizing computers and data processing, and spoke of trying to develop these new technologies from a social point of view. It had a plan to give away what amounted to 30,000,000 computer terminals, as part of a badly needed renovation of its telephone system. It was going to put all telephone books in electronic form. Then it backed off and decided to keep the paper books. It's as though they pulled the plug out of the wall.

Then France announced a mega-plan to integrate its electronics industries into a single state-backed whole. It proposed to focus on computer-aided design, manufacture of mainframe and smaller computers, the development of speech recognition technologies and the like. It insisted that, in trying to tie the whole thing together into this macro-bundle, it was merely copying Japan—which, if true, is copying precisely the wrong things. It is once again over-centralizing, and I don't give this mega-plan much hope of success.

At the same time, France is doing a number of highly publicized things to help export French computers, especially to the Third World, where the U.S. hasn't much of a lead and Japan is mainly focussing on East Asia, so far.

For example, the French have set up a very visible center for research into the applications of computing to the problems of the Third World. But the model, once again, is highly centralized. Instead of funding university research and industrial research, as might be the case in the U.S., it creates a single center for the purpose.

France is also the main sponsor, as I understand it, of the Intergovernmental Bureau of Informatics (IBI)—a group of up to 35 nations interested in spreading computers throughout the Third World. Whatever the motives, commercial or idealistic or both, it's probably a good thing.

France also has a strong position in some of the other new sciences. It has a strong ecology movement. It has a literate public.

Its real weaknesses over the long term lie in its elitist technocracy, its emphasis on nationalization, its continuing over-control of television, and its telephone monopoly. Despite these, however, France is beginning to recognize that it cannot simply reconstruct its economy on the basis of the old industries.

TECHNOPHOBIA IN GERMANY

■ You've referred to the British and French. What about the rest of Europe?

□ You can't sum up the complexity of each country's situation in so few words. But it is clear that West Germany is also caught up in the wave of economic and social restructuring we discussed earlier. After World War II, Germany rebuilt itself into the industrial society *par excellence*—standardized, centralized, synchronized and all the rest. It became a perfect crystallized example of the mass consumer, mass producer society.

It concentrated heavily on mass manufacturing—the typical Second Wave industries that are now in the deepest trouble. A report not long ago for the Ministry of Research and Technology in Bonn pointed out that the most vulnerable industries in Germany were basic metals, chemicals, mechanical engineering, rubber, etc.—precisely the industries in which Germany was historically most successful.

Today Germany has the highest unemployment in 30 years, and the collapse of AEG was the biggest near-bust since the end of the war.

Meanwhile, Germany did little to create a viable Third Wave sector. It is weak in biotechnology. It has conducted a few experiments in the new fields of communications—with videotex, for example, to deliver consumer information to the home television screen. But it has moved very slowly toward decentralization of communications· and it has a rigid, over-specialized educational system that discourages innovation, creativity or entrepreneurialism.

The German government, in fact, has contributed to mass technophobia among the young. By pushing large scale, centralized technology, by making a vast over-commitment to nuclear power for export as well as domestic use, it has fostered the impression that future technology must, of necessity, be big, centralized and inhuman. In so doing, it showed lack of sophistication. Helmut Schmidt once justified the nuclear export drive on the ground that the Americans had too big a lead in civil aircraft and computers—as though there were no other export possibilities! This export drive has advanced nuclear development in places like Argentina and South Africa.

So Germany right now is polarized. On one side you have the Second Wave establishment which thinks it can get the old industries going again or modify them, but essentially keep the old technological and social structure. Confronting them is an increasingly embittered and alienated youth that is turning backward toward a romantic, Germanic glorification of the First Wave past. It has no clear understanding of the new opportunities opened by the Third Wave.

This split in Germany is—or ought to be—unsettling to anyone who remembers Germany before the war. It could be dangerous to the rest of Europe, too, if the political situation becomes more unstable.

Fortunately, the lines aren't drawn so sharply in other countries—like Scandinavia, for example.

■ Sweden has always been a test-case for those interested in political and economic theory. Where do things stand there?

□ Because it is such a small market—after all, Sweden has only about 8,000,000 people—it hasn't been able to compete with the giants in the new high tech fields like computing. IBM still dominates the scene. Also, Swedish computers are still heavily centralized, with local governments, banks and other agencies operating central data banks and a lot of public concern over invasion of privacy. When I was in Stockholm last, I had a chance to speak with Jan Freese, director of their Data Inspection Board—a government agency that worries about the protection of privacy. It is a strong defender of individual rights, made necessary by the heavy centralism. In fact, the Swedish Defense Ministry has issued a report arguing that Sweden is militarily and socially vulnerable because of its reliance on over-centralized data systems.

But the push toward Third Wave computing—decentralization and personal computers—is already beginning, and I am sure that, from here on, it is going to move very quickly.

Sweden also expects office automation to expand fast—and there is an agreement in force between the employers and LO, the main trade union federation, governing the introduction of the new white collar technologies. In manufacturing, Sweden already has 1,000 robots in place and expects to hit 6,000-9,000 by 1990.

Sweden also has some smart corporate management. Volvo, for example, having seen the handwriting on the garage wall, has experimented with the humanization of factory work, and also, ten years ago, began to shift out of total reliance on the car business. Autos now represent only 25 per cent of Volvo's business, down from 75 per cent in 1970. What's more, Volvo aims its cars at a narrow segment of the market place—which is clever. ASEA, another big Swedish concern, is already exporting robots to—you guessed it—Japan.

So there are signs that Sweden is beginning to adapt to the Third Wave.

■ What about the Soviets?

□ We may want to get back to them later on. For now, I think we can sum up their situation in classic Marxist terms. Their system is so centralized, so stifling, so anti-innovative, not to mention undemocratic, that they are actually holding back technological development. It's a perfect example of what Marx termed a revolutionary situation—one in which the "social relations of production" prevent the further development of the "forces of production."

They think they can solve their problems by buying technology or stealing it. But their problem can't be fixed that easily.

THE AMERICAN EDGE

■ And, finally, before we come back full circle to Japan, how do you see the U.S.?

□ Despite all its problems, I still think the U.S. has tremendous advantages. It has its own natural resources, unlike Japan. It has its own oil, unlike both Japan and Europe. It has the most decentralized government of all the high technology nations. It has an educated public. Its communications are the most de-massified and advanced in the world. It has a very strong R&D base. Despite shortcomings, it has the most experience with a kind of grassroots democracy.

It also has a tradition of entrepreneurialism that makes possible the sudden success of Apple Computer, for example. It would be simply unthinkable in most of these other countries for two engineers in their mid-twenties to create a home computer, set up a company, and, in five years, build it into a household name.

Finally, and maybe most important, the U.S. has had the most experience in dealing with social, political and ethnic diversity, with sexism and racial bigotry. That doesn't mean the U.S. has even begun to solve these problems, but they are more widely discussed than in, say, Japan or most of Western Europe. Taken all together, these are plusses if you're going to move out of the traditional industrial age.

Nevertheless, I can't say any one nation is "ahead"—it's not a unilinear process. What can be said about Japan, which is where we started this discussion, is that—while it may not be facing up to its coming social, educational and cultural problems—it is facing its economic problems more consciously than the rest of us.

■ Given that, it is hard for an outsider to imagine why the Japanese feel so vulnerable.

☐ The usual answer is a set of statistics. Japan has to import 90-95 percent of its energy. It has to import about half its food. It is extremely sensitive to any ups and downs in the supply of resources. It is totally dependent on the trade system.

But I think Japan has another Achilles' heel—and here I am often in disagreement with my Japanese friends. It has to do with their racial and cultural homogeneity.

I can't count all the times I've been told by Japanese that this uniformity will help them make the transition out of the industrial age and into the new economy. Yet I see it quite differently. While homogeneity may have been an advantage in their struggle to create an industrial mass society over the past century, that is exactly the opposite of what the new society calls for. All the high tech countries are rapidly differentiating, and diversity, despite all its problems, will prove to be positive, rather than negative. The challenge that will face all of us is how to deal with rapidly rising levels of social, cultural, political, and technological diversity—not uniformity.

BEHIND THE SHOJI

■ Many describe Japan as a country without class conflict—a consensus society in which workers and employers resolve their differences harmoniously, in which workers participate in decision-making and throw themselves enthusiastically into production. How does that jibe with your own observations—and how does it relate to your view that the emerging society is likely to be de-massified?

☐ The prevailing image is, once more, superficial. There is much talk of *wakai* or reconciliation of differences, and much talk of consensus. But if the Japanese are so capable of resolving their differences peacefully, how does one explain the violent protests by farmers, students and environmentalists who almost destroyed Narita airport outside Tokyo a few years ago? Or the student protests of the 60s, or the continuing internecine violence among left-wing groups?

Once one looks behind the *shoji* panel, one finds far less consensus in Japan than outsiders suspect. Some of the older generation complain bitterly about this. Konosuke Matsushita, for example, who founded Matsushita Electric, has attacked present-day Japan because "people are badly divided and everyone pursues his own ends." And the younger generation is proving to be far more individualistic, less willing to sacrifice itself for the corporation or nation than the older generation.

As to the myth of the happy worker, labor relations at Toyota, for example, have been anything but amicable. Japanese trade unions may not be as aggressive or independent as those in the West, but the idea that they are patsies is also a myth. During the year we worked together on the television program, for example, the Japanese crew insisted on abiding by union regulations and were stickier about it than our Western sterotypes would lead one to believe.

And while class conflicts may seem muted, by our standards, there is plenty of conflict along other axes. Japan has an aggressive environmental movement. It has a consumer movement. It has plenty of quiet conflict between different industrial and financial blocs. It is simply not the conflict-free society people imagine. Which is just another way of saying it's a real society made up of real people, not stereotypes. It's filled with all the jarring differences one might expect among 118,000,000 people. Japan has serious internal problems of its own, and the notion that Europe or the U.S. should adopt Japanese management methods, or should move toward the kind of government-business cooperation that supposedly exists in Japan, is naive.

I certainly don't mean the outside world has nothing to learn from Japan. There is much to be learned—but from the real Japan, not the oversimplified card-board stereotypes that are being presented to the world. The truth is we are being hustled to adopt many of the practices that Japan today is getting ready to discard.

The Japanese know the very uncertain limits of their own success. They know that what worked for them until now may actually work against them in the future. They know that we are in a transition to some new kind of society. They are amused and flattered that we are suddenly sending missions to study them, instead of the other way around. But even this new curiosity is bounded by a profound cultural ignorance built on a sub-stratum of Western racism.

Even now, when the West, out of necessity, has suddenly taken a fresh interest in Japan, we study management systems in a narrow, export-oriented sector of the economy, but we pay little attention to Japan as a whole, its problems, its preoccupations, its politics.

I can vouch for it from personal experience. I mentioned my lectures in Japan. Well, I recently came across a reference to them in the *Asian Wall Street Journal* and it's directly germane to this discussion. It said, and I quote, "Most of Japan's business, political and academic leaders attended his lectures, which were also broadcast by a Japanese national television network." But—and here is the point—"The same can't be said about Japanese lecturers in the United States. Rarely, if ever, has a lecture by a Japanese been broadcast by an American network." And the same goes for culture. The Japanese translate hundreds, thousands of books from abroad. Despite a recent flurry, we don't take the trouble to translate many Japanese books. How many Japanese authors can Americans name? Maybe Mishima. And not because of his books. Because he was nutty enough to disembowel himself dramatically.

THE PUSH TO REARM

■ Mishima was an ultra-nationalist fascist, wasn't he? Wasn't his suicide an attempt to drum up support for a remilitarized Japan? How does that relate to the American pressure for increased military spending by the Japanese?

☐ I don't think Mishima is very important as such in this context. The fact that he formed a cult and marched into a military headquarters to kill himself is more of a curiosity than anything else. It saddens one to think that a writer of such talent could also be so psychotic. But the Mishima incident a decade or so ago ought to remind Washington that there remains in Japan a tiny, yet virulent and potentially dangerous, political group whose goal is remilitarization.

Every time Washington twists Japan's arm to spend more on warplanes or to increase the size of its navy to help patrol the Pacific sea lanes, it inadvertently lends support to this group of extremists—which, as a matter of fact, is ultra-nationalist and hence anti-American. Simultaneously, the American policy also feeds anti-Americanism among those who regard themselves as"left." And because Washington totally misunderstands Japanese culture, it exerts its pressures in a strong-arm fashion that also alienates the center-right. The result is a rising resentment that could easily explode, if trade and economic pressures worsen.

■ So you are opposed to the rearmament drive?

☐ I have said in Japan exactly what I have said in the U.S.—that if I were Japanese I would oppose the current policy of the governing Liberal-Democratic Party, which has buckled to Washington's pressure and beefed up the arms budget.

But I could also change my mind very quickly.

If I saw signs of a Chinese-Soviet rapprochement, which I regard as not impossible, I might certainly want more planes and ships.

I greatly admire Article Nine of the Japanese Constitution which is supposed to prevent the rearmament, and especially the nuclear armament, of Japan. It is a remarkable—a unique political document. I would hate to see it scrapped or diluted. But there is a world of *realpolitik* as well. And the "peace clause" was premised on U.S. economic dominance and the presence of an American military umbrella over Japan. To the degree that the U.S. military presence is weakened and U.S.-Japanese economic rivalry intensifies, it becomes harder and harder to maintain Article Nine.

DÉJÀ VU IN THE PACIFIC?

■ You seem to be hinting that someday the U.S. and Japan might actually come into military conflict in the Pacific?

□ Unfortunately, even that ghastly idea cannot be entirely dismissed. It seems utterly implausible. But I have been reading up on the early origins of the last Pacific war, and there are a number of forgotten facts worth remembering.

For example, in 1908 an American writer named Homer Lea—a proto-fascist, but brilliant and eloquent—wrote a book predicting the Pacific war that came thirty years later. In it he argued that the Pacific would eventually replace the Atlantic as the main theatre of world commerce and cultural exchange, and that economic rivalry would inevitably lead the U.S. and Japan into a collision. Tensions would be heightened by cultural misunderstanding, by conflicting moral and religious systems, and by American mistreatment of Oriental minorities—its "yellow peril" racism.

It is worth noting parenthetically that today the Pacific Basin is the fastest-growing economic region in the world, that both U.S. and Japanese capital have major investments all over the Pacific, and that census studies indicate Orientals will be the fastest growing minority group in the U.S. between now and 1995.

Lea said that America was wrong in locating the "yellow peril" in China. It was really Japan that should be feared, and he went on, in amazing detail, to describe what a Pacific war might be like. He pointed out the key strategic importance of Hawaii, the Philippines, and Alaska. He then proceeded to picture the actual landing of Japanese troops on the West Coast of the U.S., pinpointing the ports and roads they would use, which water supplies they would cut off, etc.

It was an eccentric *tour de force* intended to provoke the U.S. into increasing its military spending, and he went off the deep end. But reading it today gives one the creeps, if we recall that a decade or so later, in the 1920s, an imperialist fever was racing through Japan in preparation for its attack on China. Japan was going to "manage" all East Asia. Indonesia was going to supply its oil; Manchuria, its coal. China was going to provide a market and manpower.

By the 1930s a real trade war was raging. The Japanese, pursuing markets previously monopolized by the West, were undercutting Western prices all over the world. A GE fan, for example, sold for three times the price of a Japanese fan. Made-in-Japan cotton, cloth, glass jars, leather goods all undersold the Western products. You could buy Japanese textiles in Lancaster, England, for less than goods actually made in the Lancaster mills. You could hear the same arguments about dumping, the same calls for protectionist policies, the same racist remarks as today.

These trade wars, the deep Japanese fear that their Indonesian oil might be cut off—all contributed to World War II. The Japanese still feel vulnerable to an energy cut-off, and their entire economy is far more dependent on foreign trade than that of the U.S.

■ You're not hinting that history repeats itself, are you?

□ No. I don't trust historical analogies, and the world of today is radically different. The countries of Southeast Asia are no longer political colonies, for example. The old imperialist games don't work the way they used to. And what does all this mean in an economy which may eventually turn out to be more dependent on information than on raw commodities? And Japan itself is no longer what it was then. It is not controlled by a militarist clique. It has had a generation of post-MacArthur democratization. All the rules are changed. But to mistrust historical analogy doesn't mean we should forget the past altogether. There is an eerie *déjà vu* feeling in the air. For all these reasons, the push to rearm Japan may turn out to be a tragedy for everyone—except the Russians, against whom it is presumably directed.

The Soviets are intensifying all these pressures by moving more warships into the Pacific, thereby implicitly threatening Japan's economic life lines. But, at the same time, the build-up of Japanese arms frightens many of the surrounding nations and revives all those painful memories of Japanese imperialism. China only recently protested bitterly against a Japanese textbook that whitewashed the Japanese invasion of China.

Through the last decade, Chinese attitudes toward Japanese rearmament seemed relaxed. First, the Japanese were not rearming significantly. Second, the Chinese feared the Soviets and actually welcomed, tacitly if not openly, any increase in the power of anti-Soviet forces in the Pacific. And third, Japan was not yet the economic giant she is today. But all that is now changed.

A high Chinese official I just spoke with recalled for me the Japanese invasion of China in the 1930s. He noted that, while the militarist clique in Japan was weak in recent decades, there were other political forces in Japan who now feel that Japan is "ready" for a military role in the world. Moreover, Japan is now one of the world's premier economies. The combination of these factors has shifted the Chinese reaction, and they should give us all pause.

Another Chinese official said the key was the level of armament, and whether it was truly defensive or potentially aggressive. When I asked what would constitute aggressive arms, he didn't hesitate an instant. Nuclear weapons, medium or long-range missiles, an attack carrier, nuclear submarines—if Japan built or bought any of these, it would clearly mean, he said, that her forces were no longer for "self-defense."

Many of my Japanese friends, resentful of the pressure from Washington and worried about the deterioration of close ties between the U.S. and Japan, point out that the U.S. may be cutting its own throat, at the same time that it fosters all the worst political tendencies in Japan itself.

I once asked a highly intelligent friend of mine—an economist and international relations expert with a background in the Japanese Self-Defense Force—how he viewed the possibility of a further attenuation of U.S.-Japanese ties and a much closer alliance between Japan and China. His answer caught me by surprise.

"I would hate that," he said, "because I don't want to see the world break up into racial blocs. The close link between Japan and the U.S. crosses race lines—and that is good for us all."

His words have haunted me ever since.

■ How, then, does one sum all this up?

□ Just as we are restructuring our economic systems, we are also restructuring geopolitical relationships all over the world. The post-war structure of alliances in Europe is cracking. The Pacific is emerging as an economic power. Various high tech nations are jockeying for position in the emerging global order, each one watching its classical industries die as new ones emerge on the horizon.

Such large-scale shifts are a consequence of the rise of a new civilization, in the full sense of that term—new technologies, new economic arrangements, new social forms and, inevitably, new political structures as well. They're like the cracking and heaving of geo-tectonic plates under the earth—the upthrust of something radically new through the crust of the old order.

Until the new global structures crystallize—and that may take decades—we will continue to live with extreme instability.

4 BEYOND CAPITALISM AND SOCIALISM

The world is caught up not only in an economic and political crisis, but in an ideological crisis as well.

Whether we examine capitalist free market notions or Marxism as we have known it, whether we look at liberalism, welfare statism, or at traditional theories of Third World development—all of them seem less and less relevant as events outrace our theoretical formulations.

This ideological breakdown may be a necessary stage—a ground clearing—in preparation for the emergence of comprehensive new ideologies of the future.

Personally, I derive satisfaction from the thought that my work crosses the old ideological trenches. The Third Wave, *for example, has been favorably reviewed in the leading socialist magazines in France, published in Communist countries—yet chosen as the lead selection of the Conservative Book Club in the United States.*

It is time to put our most passionately held assumptions under the microscope. We may find that they no longer correspond to the emerging reality.

—A.T.

■ Some people reading your work or listening to you conclude that you are a right-winger; others insist you are a left-winger. You insist you are neither. Why?

□ The terms "right" and "left" are relics of the industrial period now passing into history. "Right" and "left" had to do with who got what—how the wealth and power of the industrial system were divided. But today the struggle between them is like a squabble over deck chairs on a sinking cruise liner.

Society is moving out of the industrial era so rapidly that our old political labels have become as outdated and misleading as our economic categories.

How do you label a politician—a Congressman I know, for example—who is a doctrinaire free marketeer, but who consistently supports women's rights, abortion liberalization, civil rights for minorities, environmentalism, and participationism? How do you classify supposedly left-wing activists who spout anti-semitism? Or supposedly right-wing groups who attack big business and the banks?

Are the Red Brigades rightists or leftists—or just nihilists and authoritarians using Marxist jargon as justification for their own paranoid play-acting?

And how do you describe racists who attack technocratic elites and banks, support ecology and, of all things, laetrile, and attack the medical establishment for its scientific orthodoxy? And where do you place groups that have no over-arching ideology at all, but burn with passion about a single issue? Are all anti-nuke demonstrators "left-wing"? I suspect that many of them are dyed-in-the-wool free enterprisers. Are they merely stupid, unsophisticated, unable to see that an anti-nuke position should also necessarily align them with the Third World and socialism? I don't assume they are stupid.

The attempt to range all these different phenomena on a single spectrum does violence to the many-sidedness of political life. The "left/right" terminology was always uni-dimensional. Today, it is even more distorting and obscuring than in the past.

One reason things seem so confused today is that the configuration of issues has changed—the relationships among issues, and among groups, have grown more numerous, diverse, and transient.

■ Certainly mechanical use of labels like "left" and "right," or, for that matter, "Second Wave" and "Third Wave," can be very misleading, but to make sense of issues and relationships surely they have to be grouped, even if flexibly?

□ Sure, and also placed in some order of hierarchy or priority. One of the reasons people have a hard time placing me on the spectrum is that, in my scale of priorities, the key issue is not what happens *within* industrial society, but what happens in the conflict between industrial society and the new civilization rising to challenge it. As against that historic collision, which is occurring on a world scale, all the other conflicts seem small.

On the one hand, you have those who, at all costs, want to prop up the dying industrial system. Arrayed against them are all those who are already building the next civilization.

For me, that's the super-struggle.

■ Some might say that by focussing on what you call the mega-struggle or super-struggle—this clash of civilizations, as you put it—you're diverting attention from other deep divisions separating left from right, rich from poor, powerful from powerless, and so on. Others might say, however, that your stance is compatible with being "left," as for all leftists, the tension between the status-quo and a more desirable, wholly revolutionized future is the key focus.

□ Perhaps. But what if that future also has many elements in it that the traditional "right" would admire—as, indeed, the Third Wave has? The emphasis on individualism as against mass collectivism. The re-emergence of the home as a central institution. Opposition to centralized bureaucracy. There are people on both ends of the spectrum who would share those values. But why force something to fit into pre-existent categories?

You can make a perfectly valid case there is conflict *within* any civilization. That's obvious. Sometimes between rich and poor.

Other times between various elites. And at still other times along other axes as well. I presume there will continue to be plenty of conflict in whatever new society emerges from today's changes.

But right now most people still seem unaware that the basic rules are changing, that a larger conflict has arisen that dwarfs and affects all others. We should be fighting to shape the next society, to define positions in relationship to what is emerging, not passing. This doesn't mean we ignore the immediate issues. It means reevaluating them in new terms. Politics must become more anticipatory, and positions staked out in relationship to the super-struggle.

And yes, as you say, I guess there are many leftists who would agree in the abstract, but very few who have much to say about what the future society will or should look like—and much of what they do project is essentially more of what we already have. Just more Second Wave industrialism, a bit disguised, perhaps.

And the same can be said of most "right-wingers" as well. In fact, most people, irrespective of their politics, see the future as a simple, straight line extension of the present. I think they are in for a big surprise. We've reached the end of an age—and at that point all bets are off.

The straight line future runs flat into a wall.

FORCES IN CONFLICT

■ You speak of industrialism being in "general crisis" and of powerful groups that defend "the dying industrial system," but...

☐ What we're seeing is the break-up of the system. Not the capitalist system. Not the communist system. But the industrial system that embraces both of them.

■ But when you speak of the defenders of the old system, those who you say want to preserve industrialism—what exactly do they want to preserve, and who do you see in this role?

□ Industrialism is a civilization—a social system. It's not just an economy and a political system, but a culture, a set of social institutions, an epistemology, an integrated way of life. There are people in every class, in every field, in every walk of life who have investments in that way of life. Those investments may be economic, political, psychological, sexual, cultural.

So you find giant corporations defending traditional brute force industries—like steel or textile or auto—and traditional mass manufacturing methods, including dehumanized methods of work. In fact, you often find trade unions defending the same industries and methods. You find the oil companies and the nuclear power industry defending traditional energy forms. You find certain religious groups defending the nuclear family as the only legitimate model of family life. You find the great barons of communication, whether they run the big commercial networks in the U.S. or the government-controlled networks in other countries, fighting to preserve the power of the mass media. The B.B.C.'s opposition to cable television in Britain is a perfect example. You find educators hanging on for dear life to the old models of mass education. You find politicians and parties fighting to preserve archaic political structures, most of which were designed for an agrarian or an early industrial age.

Put all these together, along with just plain ordinary people, whose jobs, egos, and status in the system depend on the continuation of that system, and you have what I call the "forces of the Second Wave."

But this great, largely unconscious coalition to defend the past is by no means a single class, race, sex, or religion. Even the poor and non-elite, even the most persecuted and powerless members of a social system or civilization may be fiercely resistant to changing it. Even they may have cultural and psychological stakes to preserve.

■ Certainly. No one can claim that every member of any particular group will go one way or another, either on a particular issue, or regarding the system-wide "super-struggle" you describe. Still, it is useful to identify groups that are more likely to swing this way or that, more likely to provide members to one side of a struggle than to the other. But if industrialism is falling apart, as you argue, what's going to replace it? Don't you need to clarify that to understand who will be for and against the changes you foresee?

□ All one can do in a few words is give a thumbnail sketch. Obviously, when I speak of a new civilization emerging, it's something I've written hundreds of pages on. After all, that's what *The Third Wave* was all about. So we can hardly expect to do the topic justice here.

But in quick summary, I'd say we are seeing revolutionary changes in all the basic subsystems that made the old industrial society hold together.

Energy—we are shifting away from exclusive dependence on fossil fuels. The conflict over this shift will, no doubt, take decades. But anyone who still pictures the energy system of, say, 2010 or 2020 as today's fossil fuel energy system writ large is making a serious mistake.

Next, production. The defining trait of industrial production is mass production. But, as I've already said, that is no longer the most advanced form. We're shifting, instead, to information-based, highly customized production and distribution of both goods and services. That has enormous implications for social and community structure, even personality development, not just economics.

Social structures? The nuclear family is no longer the dominant form. In the U.S. today, one out of five families with children is headed by a single parent. And we're seeing a multi-form family system spring up, with a diversity of structures and arrangements. It's something altogether new in history.

Corporations? Even the internal structure of these institutions is changing swiftly. It's complicated, but we are getting a shift away from classical bureaucratic forms toward more *ad hocratic* organization, smaller, more diverse units within larger modular frameworks.

Communications? We've already talked about the de-massification of the media and the rise of cable, cassette, personal computers, video, satellite, and a hundred other new media.

All these changes are moving fast, stimulating each other. And we could go into the culture, epistemology and other levels to show similar rates of change and revolutionary developments. When I speak of the Third Wave I mean all these things and more—not just economic restructuring.

Now these changes don't just happen. They happen because people make them happen. And a whole cluster of new groups are springing up whose economic, cultural, psychological and political interests lie with this emergent Third Wave system or society.

You're going to see a growing conflict between those who are fighting to make these changes in everything from industry to education and family life and those who remain totally committed to an unsustainable industrial way of life.

And here again, the basic groupings don't line up with class, race, sex, or religion, or with left and right, or with existing political parties. What's taking place is a re-configuration of the issues, themselves, and of the groups organized around those issues. There is an incipient, not yet conscious, Third Wave Movement taking shape, whether that phrase is used or not.

THE NOSTALGIACS

■ So the main conflict you see running through our time is the battle between industrialism—Second Wave society—and what you call Third Wave civilization. Where do you place developments like the ecology movement, the "Green Party" in Germany, and the anti-nuke movements around the world?

□ There are people who defend various institutions and practices of the industrial order. And there are people who attack the industrial society. They attack centralization and mega-scale, and depressing uniformity, etc. But those who attack industrialism are themselves divided.

Some of those who attack the waning industrial system are not interested in the future at all. The only alternative they can imagine is a reversion to some mythical past. They are the true nostalgiacs. I call them reversionists.

They are not Third Wave people. They glorify the First Wave past, and they may be as dangerous to our survival as the Second Wave types.

These reversionists think technology and industrialism are synonymous. They can't imagine clean technology, human technology. They make no distinction between steel mills and computers, between mass media and Xerox machines. They hate all technology indiscriminately. They don't like cities, but they fail to note that the new telecommunications are likely to help us de-urbanize. They don't like industrialism's love affair with bigness, so they come out automatically for smallness—a knee-jerk reaction.

They forget that most human beings who lived in small, rural, agricultural pre-technological settings were, in fact, the miserable victims of localist tyrannies, with no democracy, no due process in the courts, no individual rights, no contact with the outside world, no say in determining their own destiny. The reversionists, the past-glorifiers, exalt a way of life that was little more than mindless slavery for the average person.

If we want a democratic future, we had better make this distinction clear. I, for one, don't want to go back to some bucolic utopia that never existed.

It is true, and I have written at length about it, that certain emerging Third Wave forms resemble certain social and economic forms that existed in First Wave, pre-industrial societies—but now on a very high technology basis. But it is simply reactionary, in my opinion, to attack all economic development, all technology, all bigness, all centralization. It's simple-minded. It's romantic. It's melodramatic. It's futile.

I would hope that the Greens, the environmental movement, and other groups critical of industrial mass society would quit peddling despair and glorifying what was, in truth, an undemocratic past. It's time we stopped writing elegiac novels about how wonderful it was before the tin mill arrived in town. It wasn't!

Every time people lash out blindly, indiscriminately, against technology, condemning nuclear power plants and personal computers in the same breath, as though both had identical social and environmental effects, every time they mindlessly lump steel mills and tape recorders under the same loose heading "technology," they do us all a disservice. For, by urging us to burrow back toward the First Wave past, they give ammunition to the Second Wave forces who want to prevent us from moving toward a Third Wave future.

Fortunately, there are millions of people who oppose the oppression, misery, the ecological degradation and inequities of the industrial world—but who attack these from the point of view of the future, rather than some imagined past. They see the new tools—small computers, cable and direct broadcast satellite—for instance, as opening positive new options for the human race. It is these future-oriented people who are the Third Wave forces.

■ Throughout your work you speak of a historical rupture. You've argued that Marxists are wrong in attributing today's crises to the "general crisis of capitalism." But you've written little about capitalism and socialism as such.

Can capitalism or so-called "socialism" as they now exist survive the twentieth century?

□ Capitalism and socialism as we know them today? No! Each contains its own fatal contradictions. The tide of change is making them both obsolete. Contemporary capitalism and socialism are both products of the industrial revolution.

Despite the sharp differences between the two systems, industrialism gave both of them certain overriding common characteristics, precisely those structural features that are now being challenged by the Third Wave.

Just check them off against the list we ran through a moment ago. Both the capitalist and existing socialist industrial powers are dependent on fossil fuel. Mass production. Mass distribution. Mass education. Mass media. Mass entertainment. Both make the nuclear family the basic model for society. Both are built on big cities and the nation-state. Both impose the same principles of standardization, synchronization, centralization, maximization, and so forth.

These common structural features and principles are more important than the differences we usually focus on.

■ Yet you wouldn't equate the two systems?

□ No, the idea that the Soviet Union and the U.S. will somehow "converge" is based on the Second Wave belief that societies are becoming more homogenous and that is the exact opposite of what I am saying.

As to equating the systems, how can I? I'm free to state these things, to publish them without fear of prosecution. If I were a citizen of one of the so-called socialist democracies, I might well be reduced to whispering them between the bars. That's a life-and-death difference.

My books have been published, in ideologically expurgated form, in Rumania, Poland, Yugoslavia and unofficially, so to speak, in the USSR. The Soviet edition of *Future Shock*, we were told, was for limited distribution only. The woman or man on the street could not get a copy. *The Third Wave* was about to be published in Poland when the military crackdown came, and for months I could not reach my translator. The phone lines had been cut.

So I'm well aware of the life-and-death differences between these two systems.

Still, our children or grandchildren may some day look back on the great world struggle between capitalism and socialism with an amused, patronizing air—the way we now look back at the battle between the Guelphs and the Ghibellines. Throughout the 13th and 14th centuries they tore Italy apart. By the 15th century they were forgotten. Hardly anyone could remember what all the wars were about. Capitalism and socialism—and the tension between them—are products of the industrial age. When that is over, they will probably disappear as well.

■ Why do you insist so strongly that capitalism and socialism are products of the Second Wave? Certainly their beginnings can be traced further into the past than the industrial revolution?

☐ Yes, that is so, of course. Amos and Hosea in the Old Testament were crypto-socialists, for example, forever castigating the rich.

But what we call capitalism and socialism today are defined by their attitudes toward the market, and before the industrial revolution the market played a relatively small part in human history.

■ So, for you, modern capitalism and existing "socialism" are just different forms of industrial exchange-oriented society?

☐ I'd put it slightly differently: phenomena of the industrial era. Today the Soviet Union, Poland—most of the Eastern European nations—are in economic crisis. And so are the capitalist countries. The crisis is not limited to one system or the other. It's the industrial system—Second Wave civilization as a whole—that is in crisis.

■ As you well know, there are many socialists who would not call the Soviet Union or East European countries socialist at all...

☐ Of course. I'm familiar with the arguments that "real socialism"* doesn't exist, only imposters claiming the name for ideological reasons—nations that are "degenerate" versions of the real thing, or "state socialist," or whatever.

But after a century and a half of socialist theory and agitation, that's the only kind that has ever developed in an industrial society. History is telling us something. Centralized, totalitarian "socialism" may be the only kind that is possible in a Second Wave framework. It may be that industrialism *per se* is antithetical to "real socialism"—whatever that may be.

---

*Ironically, this term has diametrically different meanings in the West and in the Soviet-bloc nations. Here the word "real" is meant to suggest "ideal" or "pure" socialism. In Poland and the U.S.S.R. officials speak of the existing system as "real socialism."

Aside from which, we'd be equally justified in saying that "real capitalism" doesn't exist.

Not even the most ideological of capitalist nations today bears any resemblance to the model of pure competition. Most capitalist economies couldn't have been formed in the first place without government import quotas, restrictions, land giveaways or subsidies of one kind or another. Not to mention the fact that the big corporations often are in a position to "administer" prices in an anti-competitive way. Nor should we overlook the fact that all Second Wave governments subsidize industry by creating mass education systems that pre-adapt children for the industrial labor force. That's a gigantic hidden subvention from the public sector to the private sector.

Beyond that, there exists, in the "capitalist" nations today such a patchwork of hidden subsidies and cross-subsidies, such a contradictory pattern of permitted externalizations, that it is just as absurd to regard them as capitalist as to think of the Soviet Union as socialist.

The reality is that none of the theories works any more. Capitalist free market theories. Socialist theories. Just forget the terminology, for a moment, and look around the world. In the U.S. and Britain you have two governments committed to monetarism and free market policies, and they only manage to worsen the economic slump we're in. In Paris, a government that calls itself socialist introduces reforms that horrify Washington and London. What happens? The economy gets worse. In Eastern Europe? Bankruptcy. In the Soviet Union? Disaster. Sixty-five years after the revolution, *Pravda* admits shortages in building materials, electricity, synthetic fabrics, meat, milk, and poultry.

I just returned from Venezuela. The bulk of the economy there is run by the government. They nationalized the oil companies. The biggest bank is run by the trade unions and is subsidized by the government. Many other industries are state enterprises. And what happened? After helping start OPEC and receiving billions of dollars, Venezuela is in deep debt. It has half-built steel mills and railroads waiting to be finished. It followed a straight Second Wave development strategy and now finds itself in crisis because world oil prices are down and nobody wants more steel anyway. Public ownership didn't do very much for Venezula.

Now go south to Chile. There, Pinochet with the help of ITT and the CIA overthrows the democratically elected Allende regime and brings in Milton Friedman's disciples to help them run a real, honest-to-goodness free market economy. Friedman's "Chicago Boys" de-nationalize industry and free up the market—and the economy crashes. Bankruptcies up. Unemployment sky-high. A crisis in the banks.

Shouldn't all this begin to suggest that we're all—regardless of our ideologies (or because of them)—doing something wrong? It's so easy to blame everything on the KGB or the CIA or the left or the right or the multinational corporations or the terrorists or the Jews or the Arabs.

How can one respond with anything but irony when we hear Brezhnev use socialist rhetoric to explain why Polish workers have no right to an independent trade union? How can one react to Reagan's call for cuts in "socialistic" welfare programs so he can pump money into the Pentagon—which, together with the defense industries, just happens to form a quasi-socialist sector of the American economy?

So much for ideological purity!

CAN SOCIALISM SURVIVE CENTRAL PLANNING?

■ Let's go back to the original question—can capitalism or "socialism" in their present forms survive into the Third Wave?

You say they each contain contradictions. Socialism is supposed to resolve the contradictions of capitalism. What in your judgment is the contradiction in "socialism" as it now exists?

□ Central planning dominated by a small elite cannot work in a Third Wave society.

The industrial revolution produced a mass society. Social, political, and cultural uniformity were encouraged or imposed.

Industrialism standardized products, language, housing, education, schedules, life styles—all of which simplify things for central planners. A low-diversity society is relatively easy to run from the top.

Yet even in this relatively uncomplex system, central economic planning in large units, like nations, proved a flagrant flop wherever it was tried. It may have worked in ancient China or the Egypt of the Pharoahs. But even the most homogenous industrial economies are too complex for that kind of top-down control.

Now imagine a radically different kind of society, in which diversity, not standardization, is the order of the day. In which the mass is de-massified and also rapidly changing. Imagine not mass production, but increasingly customized production based on sophisticated technology. Imagine a world with very few smokestacks, and without millions of interchangeable workers doing repetitive work, all dressed alike, all synchronized to get up at the same hour. Imagine the disappearance of many supermarkets, and a new distribution system based on segmented marketing and individualized taste. Imagine the decline of the mass media and the appearance of direct broadcast satellite, cable, cassette, ad hoc networks, and small circulation, small audience media for every conceivable group in society, and information flooding in from every part of the world. Imagine not centralized data banks and computers, but an Apple or TRS-80 in every kitchen, all linked up in ever-changing networks. That's more like where we're headed and it's a nightmare for central planners.

That kind of society is much harder to control from the top. The "decision load" of the planners becomes literally unmanageable.

Here's the key: the more diverse or differentiated any society becomes, the more the local conditions vary, the faster the changes become, the more variation there is from moment to moment. And the Third Wave brings both these processes—diversification and acceleration.

Central planners are forced to deal in trends—in broad generalized decisions. They can't turn out flexible, customized decisions, tailored to local or short-term conditions. They don't know enough about what's going on in each specific location, and if they try to find out, they usually can't.

You can't make good decisions unless you can continually monitor their effects. For this you need people who are located on the periphery to tell you what's happening. You need information and you need it on time. You most especially need information about your errors. It's called negative feedback.

But that's the last thing you, as a central planner, want to hear. You're always afraid your boss will punish you. Whole careers are built on denying error.

So the people down below, not being stupid, sugar coat the information or just plain lie, or send in the truth too late, or play any number of other games with the information.

Why not? If they can't participate in making a decision, or setting quotas, and have no responsibility for the decision, it's better to tell you what you want to hear or, better yet, tell you as little as possible. Or, alternatively, drown you in useless information. They have no control over how the information will be used. It might even be used against their best interests.

At a minimum, the central planner must have multiple, parallel channels of information extending into every capillary of the system under control, and he or she needs internal devil's advocates, whistle-blowers, critics and nay-sayers who have nothing to lose by talking back. But I know of no centrally planned economy in which anything remotely like this exists—and for obvious reasons. Any such system, honestly run, poses a continuing threat to the central planner.

So the central planner in a non-participatory system lives in a world of lies, illusions and anachronisms—and whole economies can be wrecked as a result, and, indeed, have been. History is littered with stupid decisions made by quite intelligent central planners.

■ As you know, many in today's radical left have no love for technocratic central planning. But what is to prevent the centrally planned economies being forced by internal pressures to open up more democratic channels of communication—with workers, consumers, ethnic minorities, women and the community at large? Wasn't Solidarity trying to push Poland in that direction, and perhaps even further, toward a more participatory planning system in which communication doesn't always have to go through a center but might go sideways, from participant to participant, instead?

☐ Some members of Solidarity were. Others assuredly were not. Clearly it is *conceivable* that pressure from below could force changes in the central planning machinery of Eastern Europe or the Soviet Union. But in most of these countries the bureaucratic and party resistance is so entrenched that it would require little short of a political revolution to bring it about. Moreover, so long as these countries remain primarily industrial or Second Wave nations, the pressures toward centralization will remain strong. I can imagine Solidarity, for example, replacing the military regime with a more democratic one—but still attempting to plan the economy from the top down.

As to the more general possibilities for democratic, participatory planning, you may be able to do this on a small, quite local scale, but, even if you wanted to, it is almost impossible in a traditional mass society. More important, it's not in the short-term self-interest of the central planning elites to do so. Finally, even where the central planners would like to democratize the system, opening up the channels for feedback threatens to drown the planners in undigested and even indigestible local detail.

I don't care how intelligent the planners are, how many Ph.D.'s they hire, or how good they are at delegating, or how big their computers are. At some point, in the high-diversity, fast-change environment we live in, they're overwhelmed. The people at the center have to make too many decisions about too many things they can't possibly understand.

■ So you're saying the more the Third Wave brings diversity into the economic and social system, the harder it is going to be for anyone to manage the system centrally?

□ Right. The real solution is not merely to open up channels through which citizens or consumers, workers, and others can feed information up to the decision-makers. The real solution is to redistribute the decision load, itself, so that more discretion, more power to take certain decisions, is transferred down below. Some also will have to be transferred up out of the nation-state to new transnational agencies—but that's another topic.

The point is that if the present centrally-planned economies actually do transfer substantial decision-making downward—and there's no evidence the entrenched elites in the Soviet Union and other centrally-planned economies are ready to do this without a bitter struggle—if they do actually carry out a change, and permit significantly more local autonomy, they will no longer be centrally planned in the sense we are discussing.

The Third Wave threatens to bring this crisis to a head in all the Soviet-style nations. The Third Wave threatens to engulf the planners under the sheer weight of information.

■ There are many leftists, I believe, who would agree, adding an ethical plea in favor of people exercising greater direct control over their lives as an additional argument against central planning. Indeed, there are those who feel that real socialist economics is precisely about the need to create ways of organizing economies so people can self-consciously directly control their own economic lives, rather than having coordination occur by way of either the market or through top-down planning mechanisms. But, beyond these structural concerns, what about the human element—the attitudes of people themselves?

□ There you find an even deeper contradiction between what the central planners call socialism and the kind of society that is now emerging—a really explosive political and social contradiction.

Socialism was supposed to produce a new kind of person. Well, I don't know about socialism, but it certainly takes a completely different kind of worker to make the Third Wave economy run— not a member of the "masses," but an individual. It takes resourceful, educated, independent, risk-taking, creative workers—and that's precisely the kind of person the Soviet elites can't tolerate.

This is what I meant before by the statement that the "social relations of production" in the Soviet Union are standing in the way of the development of the "forces of production." I use those Marxist terms precisely because it's language they, themselves, might understand.

They want the advantage of an up-to-date Third Wave society, but they can't afford to allow the diversity and freedom necessary for it to develop. So they've tried to solve the dilemma by buying new technology from outside. But this is simple-minded. It reflects the Marxist's overestimation of material factors. Technology by itself can't bring the Third Wave. A Third Wave economy requires a Third Wave culture and a Third Wave political frame.

This suggests to me that they will have to decentralize and democratize eventually, whether they want to or not. They'll have to permit error, to permit negative feedback. It means allowing not one, but 100 Solidarities to spring up. In short, if they want the benefits of an advanced economy, they'll have to transform their entire system.

The contradictions will blow their system apart unless they adapt to the Third Wave.

PROPERTY: A LEFT-WING OBSESSION

■ What about capitalism? You say the Third Wave is incompatible with the kind of oppressive central control that you find in the Soviet Union today and in the other existing "socialist" societies as well. But one of the most fundamental characteristics of capitalism is that an exceptionally small number of people own the great bulk of the means of production. Another very small group, many of whom overlap the economic ruling class, occupy the highest reaches of political power. Can this hierarchical system last? And if not, where is its "fatal" contradiction?

◻ The contradiction lies at the very heart of capitalism—in the concept of private property. Left-wingers are so obsessed with the idea of property—ownership—that they are often blinded to the actual facts of the matter. The very concept of property is turning itself inside out.

The people who dominate advanced "capitalist" societies today are not necessarily those who "own" the means of production.

Increasingly, the people who dominate do so because they control the means of integration—they are the managers. In the U.S., which is supposed to be the heart of world capitalism, property has been losing its significance for a generation.

Basic decisions about the future of our society in the United States have been, and are being, made by business executives who often have no ownership of capital or of machines, whatever. Key decisions are also made by underpaid government bureaucrats who decide that an investment is going to go to this region or that one, or to this technology or that one. Some of their decisions are far more important than those of stockholders.

There are exceptions, of course—large companies that are still family-controlled, or in which a small stockholding group *does* exercise control. You and I can both name some big companies that are still controlled by owners.

But if we look at the really major enterprises, the ones around which the economy pivots, we find relatively little owner control. If anything, we find pension funds, some of them owned or co-managed by unions.

Naturally, this varies by country, and, in some, private ownership of the dominant enterprises remains a reality. Not long ago I spoke at the Royal Swedish Academy of Engineering Sciences to an audience of conservative Swedish businessmen, engineers and scientists. It was an unusual auditorium, because it was wired up for instant polling of the audience. So I took the opportunity to ask *them* some questions, including whether, in their opinion, ownership of Swedish industry was concentrated in too few hands. To my—and their—surprise, fully 90 percent answered "yes" to that question. So I wouldn't wish to over-generalize from American experience, nor to quibble about precise definitions of "concentration of ownership."

The basic question is who makes the big decisions. And in many countries it is clear that managers, rather than owners as such, are determining the direction of investment and business policy.

My old teacher James Burnham, in *The Managerial Revolution*, and A. A. Berle, Jr., in *Power Without Property*, pinpointed this trend decades ago. Galbraith in his discussion of the "technostructure" provides a better map of the reality than the Marxist who still thinks she or he can understand major corporate decisions simply by tracing ownership patterns and assuming that corporations are narrowly driven by the maximization of profit.

If we want to understand how power is likely to be distributed in the future, we need to look more closely at what constitutes property and how the Third Wave transforms it.

■ Certainly managers, bureaucrats, and administrators make important decisions. And they undoubtedly have interests of their own, in addition to seeking profit in compliance with market and owner pressures. But it is also true, isn't it, that in a corporate market framework, companies pursue profit to retain market shares, finance investment and otherwise preserve their economic positions? And even in cases where the interests of managers and owners may be opposed, doesn't the context still lead to anti-social decisions in tune with the interests of the latter?

□ That same context may lead to very positive decisions that benefit society, as well as anti-social decisions. There is no question that many corporate policies—both good and bad—result from a frenetic search for "bottom line" results in the short term. The price of the company's stock clearly operates as a factor in decision-making, and no responsible executive is going to make decisions to damage the stock or the company's market position.

But the very large companies, especially where they are diversified, are often engaged in so many different operations that no one operation by itself affects the stockholders' results markedly.

Investors complain they can't get a "pure play."

The decision to market a new line of soap or a new kind of shirt, or even a nuclear reactor, often bears little relationship to the return received by the actual stockholder.

So what becomes steadily more important is decisional power and control, not ownership.

I don't mean to push this too far. There was a time when ownership of something did mean active control of the key decisions. And that's still true in thousands of small enterprises. But they are hardly the ones that dominate.

In fact, to focus on ownership is to ask the wrong question. It is essentially a First or Second Wave question. All left-wing analysis starts from the Marxist obsession with ownership, which made sense a hundred years ago, but is now becoming progressively less relevant.

In First Wave societies, the only property that meant much was land.

In Second Wave societies, the essential property was no longer land, but ownership of the "means of production"—the machines on the GM assembly line, the factories, etc.

Ownership in the capitalist industrial nations, moreover, took the form of share ownership—in which you held a piece of paper. That paper was already a symbolic abstraction from reality. It symbolized a piece of a building or a piece of a machine. But it at least still had a material basis.

In the supposedly socialist countries, ownership was largely state ownership, and the symbol of your ownership, theoretically, was the fact that you were a citizen. As a citizen, you held one two-hundred-millionth share in the economy, and that supposedly mattered. But here, too, the property that counted was tangible—machines, equipment, and buildings.

In a Third Wave society, we still need land and hardware, but the essential property becomes information, and that, as I've already pointed out, is a revolutionary switch because it's the first form of property that is non-material, non-tangible, and potentially infinite.

If I own a share of IBM today (which I don't), what do I really care about? What do I own? I don't care a rap about Yorktown Heights, the land on which IBM has some buildings. I don't care about its plants in San Jose, California, or Bogotà, Colombia. I don't care about the buildings or even machines. What I really care about is the organized information it controls.

My property is now doubly abstracted from reality. A share of IBM is a piece of paper—a symbol. And beyond that, it's a symbol not of hardware or real estate. It's a symbol of other symbols inside people's heads.

Finally, as I pointed out earlier, "info-property" is distinct from "real property" in that it is not finite. I can use it, and you can use it at the same time. And, in fact, the more people who do use it, the more information is likely to be generated.

So property simply isn't what it used to be when Marx and the early socialists built their theories on it.

This is the fatal contradiction I spoke of. Private property has been the defining characteristic of capitalism. Now suddenly the essential property transforms from symbolic to meta-symbolic, and from finite to non-finite in character. And that contradicts the very notion of property which has been based on its scarcity and materiality.

■ Of course, you know that many Marxists and socialists have left behind a single-minded focus on ownership relations to concentrate on other social relations as well.

□ Perhaps. But property remains an obsession for many, despite the fact that new developments and the rise of the Third Wave make ideological goulash out of all old economic theories—capitalist and socialist alike.

Capitalism and socialism are both anachronisms.

5 INFO-POLITICS

Will tomorrow bring less or more democracy? The answer is not pre-ordained. It depends, at least in part, upon our own actions. But to understand the prospects for democracy, we need to understand the new role of information in our political life.

The rapid emergence of a new society focusses attention on a whole range of political issues having to do with information. Privacy in the age of the computer. Satellite transmission of information across national boundaries. Data protectionism. Copyright. Freedom of information. These are only the visible tip of the new problems confronting us. Underlying them are more profound questions with long-range implications for democracy.

Throughout our discussions, the talk kept returning to information and the political role of those who process, manipulate, or create it: the "mind-workers."

—A.T.

■ Millions of words have been written about the information revolution. But very little analysis has been devoted to its causes. Why, in your opinion, are we now entering what some call the "information age"? Why not 100 years ago, or, for that matter, 100 years from now?

☐ Social causation is complicated, but I think we can identify at least some of the forces that account for the information revolution. We can make it comprehensible.

For me, the fuel of the information revolution is a combustive mixture of diversity and accelerated change. Put them together and you produce an information explosion.

Since approximately the mid-1950s we've been experiencing the crack-up of the old industrial mass society. In scores of fields, from technology to ethnicity, we see greater and greater diversity. As the Third Wave arrives on the historical scene, it creates a new civilization which is composed of more differentiated, more specialized parts.

Imagine a simple biological organism—an earthworm for example. It has few differentiated parts. Contrast that with a human—we have lungs and kidneys and corneas and a cortex and thousands of interrelated, functionally specialized parts. For all these parts to interact properly, a vast amount of information has to flow through the body in the form of electrical pulses, chemical bursts, hormonal secretions, each of which represents a "message"—so that a certain neural pulse, for example, tells the muscle to contract or the pupil of the eye to dilate. These "messages" contain "information" and tremendous amounts of information need to be routed through the body if its parts are to be coordinated and synchronized with one another.

And the more specialized or diverse the parts of the body, the more information is needed. There's more information flowing through our bodies than through the body of that earthworm.

Now let's apply the same principle to society.

If I'm right that we're moving beyond the stage of mass production, distribution, and communication; if the division of labor is becoming even more refined; if the variety of organizational structures is increasing; if we are moving toward smaller, more numerous, more decentralized units (sometimes organized within very large organizational frameworks); if our laws are multiplying and our products, values and attitudes becoming more hetero- geneous; if all this is happening, then it takes far more information merely to keep the whole system in equilibrium.

In short, the heterogeneity of the Third Wave society demands higher levels of information exchange than the homogeneity of Second Wave society.

■ You have diversity generating information. But doesn't that put the cart before the horse—in the sense that the information may also generate diversity?

☐ Absolutely. There's what the engineers would call a positive feedback loop. Cable television, for example, permits more varied symbols and messages to flow through society—more information. This encourages greater social diversity. Diversity, in turn, raises the level of information needed for social coordination and integration. So, in one sense, you have diversity feeding on itself, and continually raising the levels of information needed in the system.

But there's another factor that is often overlooked, and that's the speed of change, itself. The faster things change, the more information we need to deal with it. It's really just a special case of the principle I mentioned a moment ago, because change can be regarded as diversity in time. The state of being at one moment becomes different the next. And the more often that happens, the more information we need to keep on making adaptive decisions.

So I see rising diversity combined with rapid change as the basic reasons we are experiencing an information explosion.

The society is evolving from earthworm to human being, as it were, and the transformation is occurring at very high speed— faster than the agricultural revolution of 10,000 years ago or the industrial revolution of 300 years ago.

■ And how does this leap to a higher level of information exchange materially affect us?

□ If you look at employment in all the industrial societies, from Belgium or Britain to Japan and the United States, you find a relentless decline in manual labor and a parallel rise in white-collar work ever since the mid-50s.

The system has gotten so internally complex and diversified, and the informational demands so high, that they have begun to reach a crisis point.

It requires so much paperwork, so much coordination, so many meetings and decisions, so much information exchange to get anything done, that we literally face the risk of grinding to a halt. That's why white-collar jobs have been increasing in recent decades.

Starting a decade or two ago, nobody could contain it any more. The paperwork began to overflow all our channels of communication. And as this pressure rose toward the bursting point, the system began to respond technologically. Computers, originally designed for scientific calculation, were adapted to handle simple administrative tasks. They spread into offices everywhere.

Communications channels laid in place during the industrial era—telephone systems, for example—were overloaded, unprepared to handle the new flood of computerized data. So over the past two decades we've seen a plethora of new communications channels opened up, and new tools for handling data have also emerged—word processors, optical scanners, microfilm storage, and hundreds of related technologies—a burst of innovation aimed at lightening the information overload.

So we can trace a cycle: more diversity and change equals more information equals more technologies to handle information—and that, I suspect, leads to still more diversity and change.

That's the dynamic driving the information revolution, which is only part of the larger wave of change now beginning to obliterate the old industrial society.

Furthermore, as we increase and organize all this additional information, we also deepen our scientific understanding of nature, so that we begin to transform the very processes of production. Instead of using a lot of manual assembly to make, say, a camera or a television set, we use more information and deeper knowledge to reduce the number of parts. We inject information, as it were, into the machine itself. And all this has effects not only on the economy, but on the culture, too.

■ In what way does the information revolution affect the culture?

□ During the industrial age, our main concerns were how to make things. Now our primary concerns become how to manage things. We begin to make more use of information analogies—like the one I just used a moment ago about the body. We begin to analyze problems in terms of information theory. We begin to shift from behaviorist explanations in psychology to cognitive explanations. In Marxist theory, we see an increased interest in Gramsci* and an emphasis on problems of culture, ideology, epistemology. In politics, as I've already suggested, issues of the control of information, privacy, the management of information flow, become more and more important. They even take on a global dimension as countries battle over things like the proposed New International Information Order. "Meta-information" becomes the key to control in every field.

   The old idea that knowledge is power is now obsolete. To achieve power today you need knowledge about knowledge.

WHO WILL RUN THE INFORMATION SOCIETY?

■ That brings us to power—which is what politics is all about. You suggest that the emerging Third Wave society will be more democratic than the industrial order.

□ Could be, not "will be."

---

*Antonio Gramsci (1891-1937), Italian Communist thinker whose works examine the role of intellectuals and culture in political and social change.

■ But couldn't we go in the other direction, even perhaps toward a kind of 1984ish techno-fascism? Or more likely, mightn't the shift to the Third Wave, and especially the information revolution which is part of it, change the class structure of our society, not toward more equity, but toward a new hierarchy, the knowledge-priests on top, the rest holding up the pyramid?

□ Some of the new technologies are certainly threatening. But others are the reverse—they enhance the power of the individual vis-à-vis the state. They're not the same. Some are centralist, others decentralist. It's a mistake to lump them. Smart politics would restrict the use of one type and greatly encourage the spread of the other, thus not only foreclosing any possibility of "techno-fascism" but also promoting a new level of democracy.

Let me give you a few concrete examples. The most powerful communications tools of the industrial age were the mass media—controlled from the center either by government or by big companies. Contrast that with, say, a tape recorder, which is used by the consumer and can be employed to make messages, to pass them along, duplicate and reduplicate them. This is what the Soviet dissidents did to escape the ear of Big Brother. It is also what the anti-shah rebels did in Iran. The tape recorder can't be centrally controlled.

Or take the Xerox machine, which can be used to publish illicit ideas. The Russians try to lock them up, but as the machines proliferate it gets harder and harder.

Or take the computer. The first ones: centralized and enhancing the power of the government or corporate user. The new ones: small enough to be used by anyone, even kids.

Or take cable television as compared with broadcast media. The old system: one way. The new system: interactive, so that viewers can talk back to the sender.

One could go on to show the appearance of all sorts of new technologies, especially in information and communication fields, that could help reduce central control over our lives, rather than increase it.

The other question you raise is equally interesting—the question of class relationships...

■ Aren't we creating a new class of technocrats—professionals, managers, scientists, and computer people? And mightn't the emergence of this new economic class have implications for the rest of us?

In broad strokes couldn't we say that until now we've had, in the West, a capitalist class, a working class, and a small class of "technocratic types" who ran things for the capitalists (and also had interests of their own)?

With the increasing importance of information, isn't this third class growing in size and power? Isn't there a clear danger, in your view, that instead of a democracy we will wind up with a technocracy in which political power is monopolized by this third class?

☐ I have trouble with the very concept of "class." If we speak of "classes" in the strict Marxist sense, then we define them in terms of their relationship to the "means of production"—i.e., ownership. The bourgeoisie was supposed to own the means of production; the proletariat was supposed to own nothing but its labor power—essentially its muscles.

I've already said that in today's world ownership is not necessarily related to control. Which is especially interesting if we remember that Marx, himself, had a lot of trouble with the notion of ownership in non-industrial societies. In many of these, power came not from actually owning the land, but from serving as the monarch's representative in a particular locality, and getting a stipend or rake-off for it. It was "pre-bendal" property.

A lot of writers, from Max Weber to George Konrad and Ivan Szelenyi, have argued that actual ownership was seldom the key to power before the industrial age, that the idea of class based on ownership simply didn't fit the realities of non-industrial societies.

Well, as I see it, we are moving once more into a non-industrial society, only now, based on high technology. So that the relative importance of ownership diminishes once more. It's a dialectical process. If Marx were around today, he might have gotten a good laugh out of this irony!

■ But what about this new class? Ownership, after all, is not the only basis for defining class, and this one, clearly, is based more on role, type of work, training, etc.

□ If the Second Wave gave us a "proletariat," we might say that the Third Wave is producing a "cognitariat"—a group based on knowing, on the use of mind, rather than on muscle.

The cognitariat possesses organized information, imagination, and other cultural qualities essential for production. It owns the means for the production of more information. It owns what might be regarded as either an essential raw material or, alternatively, a kit of mental tools. So it comes to the bargaining table with more power than the proletariat ever did.

But the real question is whether it's right to think in such strictly economic terms. We might more usefully think of this group as a social class—or even better as a cultural class. Its economic significance may be secondary.

■ But if this group increases from, say, 10,000,000 to 30,000,000 people—the numbers are just hypothetical—does that necessarily give us a future society based on real economic freedom or participatory democracy?

□ No. But it can be argued that because the information inside its collective brain is essential to the economy, this group is crucial. And if it ever becomes the majority, it will stand in a new relationship to the state.

After all, almost by definition this group is relatively well-educated, worldly, and sophisticated. It has access to advanced communications. It has its own 'media—thousands of specialized publications, tapes, and computer networks. It is by no means powerless vis-à-vis either the capitalist owners or the state. In this sense the cognitariat is in a quite different position from that of the proletariat.

■ You don't think—nor even hope—that everyone will eventually be a member of this new "cognitariat"?

☐ No. Not everyone can—or should—be a member of the cognitariat. I believe the general level of sophistication in society is likely to rise, and that the so-called "stupidity problem" is smaller than most of us like to think. It makes some people feel good to regard the rest of the human race as essentially uneducable.

But I certainly don't assume that everyone is equipped—or can be equipped—with the rather specialized mental skills required for mind-work. What mind-workers need is a talent for abstract reasoning and articulation. And not all of us are good at it. It isn't even a matter of intelligence. Some highly intelligent people aren't very articulate. And we don't know enough about abstract reasoning— at least I don't—to equate that with general intelligence.

The fact is that even those who work with information—i.e., in a world of abstractions—will also want to return frequently to the world of concrete experience. This means direct involvement with others. It means body care and health care. It means tactile, sensory involvement with the environment through things like manual activity, gardening, cooking, sailing, or, for that matter, touch-football, dance, or construction—building a home or a cabin in the mountains, for example.

All this means, in turn, a great many jobs and roles in society for people who might not fare well in a world of high abstraction. So not everyone will be a mind-worker.

■ Perhaps the reason some people won't feel comfortable with "mind-work" will be that they haven't the training or that, knowing there would be a shortage of "mind-work" job opportunities, they have socialized themselves, so to speak, to want the kind of work they will actually have access to. But whatever the cause, if some do "mind-work" while others do more traditional types of labor, won't the mind-workers dominate the new society? Won't political parties emerge to extend the interests of this group, as against the interests of the owners and non-information workers? Won't the cognitariat's relative monopoly on "mind-work" give it immense advantages in any contest for social impact? And what about people who still do manual labor, or provide face-to-face human services?

☐ We may be asking the wrong questions. The rise of this cognitariat is directly connected with the process of differentiation in society. If you didn't have increasing diversity, you wouldn't need and wouldn't have so large a class of coordinators, technicians, knowledge handlers and manipulators.

But precisely because we are now getting higher diversity it's a mistake to assume mind-workers will act as a "mass"—as a unified bloc.

It is precisely these people who are most associated with the rise of single issue groups in politics, with the anti-nuke campaign, with the battles over abortion law, and with many other highly particularized goals. They both reflect and promote the new social and political diversity.

Marx argued that the factory system created the conditions for the unity of the working class. I would argue that the end of the factory system, in its traditional form, and the shift to de-massified production and distribution, creates counter-conditions—they lay the base for de-massified political movements. And that's what we are getting.

The idea that the mind-workers will unite to oppress the rest of society is, I believe, wrong. They may have a harder time forming a unified majority than any other group.

THE DECISIONAL ENVIRONMENT

■ So you think the rise of the mind-worker will finally mean more democracy?

☐ There is, in fact, a way of looking at democracy itself as a function of information and decision-making in society. Of course, politics is more than just a decision system. It is a form of theater. It is a game. It is very often a form of religion. But it is also the process by which we make many of our most important collective decisions. So its decisional aspect is crucial. And although I've been personally identified with the movement to expand citizen participation, to develop new democratic forms, one of the more somber thoughts you'll find in *The Third Wave* is that there may be limits to the number of people who can, at any given moment, participate in decision-making in society...limits, that is, to democratic participation.

■ What kind of decision-making are you talking about?

☐ I'm not referring to private decisions that only affect ourselves and perhaps a few people close to us. I'm speaking of what might be called social decision-making, which would include economic and political decisions. When we speak of participation and democracy, those are the kinds of decisions we mean.

■ The limits you refer to—don't they make it possible for technocrats to seize all decision-making power? And if not, how will the rise of this new class of mind-workers, as you call them, affect the political process?

☐ If I want to know that the political future may be, in a highly de-massified society with a large group of information workers or processors, it helps me to look backward before I look forward.

One of the things that seems clear is that pre-industrial societies were also pre-democratic.

In older agricultural societies, damn few people ever participated in making the basic political or economic decisions. Historically, agriculture has seldom been a friend to democracy. Even Athens, the counterexample, was democracy for the few based on slavery for the many. One way or another, a small, authoritarian ruling class usually dominates any agricultural society.

It was industrialization that brought what we call democracy. Along with the wave of industrialization came explosive democratic revolutions and reforms that led to a broadening of participation.

One thing seems clear to me. It takes a lot more decision-making to run an industrial society than a pre-technological agricultural society. In the old agricultural societies, a handful of barons, their assorted relatives, a few local priests—they constituted the group that made all the basic socioeconomic and political decisions for the entire community. It doesn't take many decisions to run a feudal plantation or manor. Ninety per cent of the people were peasants who had neither the right, the education, nor, very often, the desire to participate in making those decisions.

Now suddenly along comes the industrial revolution, and instead of a simple decentralized economy, you now have a complex, interdependent economy and society in which very different activities must be coordinated. What happens is that the sheer quantity and quality of the decision-making changes. It takes more interrelated decisions to run an industrial society than a pre-industrial society.

You know, we all recognize that if you change the physical environment by destroying the carrying-capacity of the land, or by flooding a river basin, the people in that environment may have to reorganize themselves to survive. The structure of any society responds to changes in the physical and technological environment, as well as to changes in the the strategic, economic, and cultural environment.

Well there is also an invisible *decisional environment*. And societies respond to changes in that, too. What the industrial revolution did, among so many other things, was to dramatically alter the decisional environment.

SPREADING THE DECISION LOAD

■ And how do changes in the decisional environment affect the political environment?

□ It's important to grasp the concept of a decision load.

At any given moment, there is a certain burden of decision-making that is required to run any society—a certain number of decisions of a certain degree of complexity to be made within a given interval of time.

As the Second Wave rolled over the old First Wave agricultural order, it brought with it not only smokestacks, but a much greater need for coordination and integration, all of which required many more decisions than ever before. In turn, this led to a sharp growth in the percentage of people involved in making decisions—in business, in politics, in community life. This group was organized into a hierarchy of elites and sub-elites, and formed the backbone of the middle class.

To put it differently, the arrival of industrialism radically increased society's decision load.

The tiny elites of the past could no longer make all the decisions required to run the new society. So additional decision-makers were recruited. And instead of a tiny, closed, hereditary elite, you got a much larger, more open system of elites and sub-elites which came into being to handle the expanded decision load. This is the essence of the "democratic revolution" that came along with the industrial revolution—the involvement of more people in the decision-making process.

■ You speak as though everyone benefited—as though there were real democracy. But, in fact, only a minority participated in making all the decisions, in handling what you call the decision load.

□ That's true. The spread of democracy never embraced everyone.

The middle classes got good slots in the new structure of decision making. The workers and farmers, who were recruited to fight for democratic reforms, got, as their pay-off, the right to vote intermittently.

That's a limited form of participation. But the fundamental everyday decisions were basically made without any real participation by workers and farmers, and, by and large, they still are. Partial democracy—call it semi-democracy—came when there was a sudden increase in the society's decision load.

Now the decision load is expanding again. That makes this a crucial moment in political history.

■ You aren't suggesting, are you, that the working class and the farmers are suddenly going to gain power in the system? That suddenly we're going to get a truly participatory democracy?

□ No. Not at all. In fact these groups may dwindle in size and significance. In the United States, today, only four per cent of the population are farmers. The number of manufacturing workers may eventually approach that as well. The key question is what happens next.

Three things are going to affect our political future. One is the increase in mind-workers. The second is a new, staggering jump in the decision load. And the third is the computer.

If I'm right that we are de-massifying the whole society, from energy and production to family life and values, then even more information is going to pulse through the society, and that means more information workers and more decisions. It also means that the present ruling elites and sub-elites will not be able to handle the decision load by themselves, any more than the feudal elites at the time of the industrial revolution.

In fact, if I look around I see highly intelligent men and women making stupider and stupider decisions—in politics, in industry, in investment, in education, in every field. The quality of our decision-making is deteriorating across the board. Not because the people in charge are stupid. But because they're all running too fast, making too many decisions, too fast, about too many things they know too little about.

Our managerial elites are staggering under an impossible decision load. That will force the elites to allow more people to participate—to help carry the decision load. That's why we hear more and more about participatory management—more and more about involving the workers. Not because of altruism, but because the old decision system doesn't work.

Politically, this suggests more public involvement, too. Call it a further expansion of the middle class. Call it broadened democracy. Call it participation. Whatever you call it, it means more people are drawn into decision-making, fewer are totally excluded.

■ There are decisions, and then there are decisions.

□ Yes. I'm not suggesting that large numbers will necessarily participate in making the key decisions. Most of us will be drawn into making low-level, everyday decisions of the kind needed to keep businesses, communities, or organizations operating—the scut-work of decision-making.

But that gives people at least some stake in the system, some identity, some status. It should in no way be sneered at.

■ I'm not sure I'd call that an expansion of democracy—more like token rights handed out to keep the ship afloat. And couldn't it be consistent with a kind of technocracy?

□ Use whatever terms you want. Still, the fact is that the percentage of people who are totally left out of social, organizational and political decision-making, at some level or other, is reduced when the decision load gets too heavy for the existing elites to handle by themselves.

I also don't mean to suggest that all this happens without conflict. In fact, I anticipate tremendous conflicts over the right to participate.

New openings in the decision structure—the doorways into the sub-elites and elites—are not available to everyone on equal terms. The elites still tend to apply criteria that work against certain groups—women, blacks, and Hispanics have a harder time in the United States than other groups. Some manage to join the ranks of decision-makers. But it's harder for them because of racism and sexism. In other countries, other forms of discrimination come into play.

But the key idea is that the structure of society—its complexity, diversity, and rate of change—determines its decision load. This, in turn, has powerful effects on the structure of elites and sub-elites who essentially run things by making decisions. Information is closely correlated with power and with politics—and will become even more so as we move into the era of "info-politics."

THE COMPUTER IN POLITICS

■ Where does computer technology fit into all this?

☐ The computer has an incredible number of impacts on the political system. Big, tightly centralized computer systems increase the power of the state over the individual. But small, decentralized computers and computer networks can be used to strengthen individual power. Computers radically alter the military strategic balance, political polling, even the way political issues get defined. Computers make possible the kind of very closely targeted mailings now used by political groups in the United States, thereby contributing to the rise of single issue groups. I could go on and list many other political implications of the computer. But it also relates back to the theory of decision load.

The computer was originally viewed by the elites as a machine that would reduce their decision load and help them cope. They saw it as a means of centralizing their control and making many routine decisions automatically, thereby freeing them to make higher-level decisions and maintain control. It also meant they could continue to do their jobs without recruiting large numbers of additional decision-makers.

What's happened so far doesn't bear out their hopes. The decisional load, if anything, has continued to grow rapidly since the introduction of the computer. In fact, it's grown so fast that more and more decision-making has had to be decentralized, with the result that computers are now cropping up in places the old elites could never imagine. Instead of a few giant computers controlled from the top down, we are getting hundreds of thousands, eventually millions of computers, spread through the society, in homes and schools and churches and garages, linked up in transient networks, out of the control of any central computer.

The overall result, I believe, could ultimately be an increase, rather than a decrease, in the percentage of people involved in social, economic and political decision-making. The computer could—I emphasize could—be the most important friend of democracy since the ballot box. It could also be turned against us.

■ But even if your theory is right, there are still limits on who can or will participate. What happens, in your view, to those who are not part of the new class of knowledge workers, coordinators, and integrators?

☐ That remains the 256K-bit question.

In societies still heavily impregnated with racism, sexism, religious bigotry, and xenophobia in general, disadvantaged groups will have to fight for every step, every opening in the decision-structure.

■ What you have sketched, whether one agrees with it or not, is a theory of politics for the information age. Even your key concepts, like "decision load," refer to information and its uses. But none of that, as you yourself suggest, necessarily eliminates such cultural and political factors as racism and sexism. How do they fit into your view of the politics of tomorrow?

☐ Let's focus on that next.

6 THE REVOLUTION IN ROLES

Why, after millions of years of development, is the human race still plagued by the diseases of sexism and racism?

Roughly speaking, sexism and racism are beliefs that justify the domination of one sex or race over another.

To use these terms is not to suggest that men and women are identical or that racial distinctions are insignificant. But there is a big difference between recognizing human diversity—and constructing or tolerating systems of oppression based on that diversity.

Unfortunately, the human race has shown enormous relish and inventiveness when it comes to justifying oppression. All sorts of theories—involving everything from intelligence to art, from economics to crime—have been cooked up to rationalize the mistreatment of minority groups and women.

In the new society that is emerging we will all be members minority groups. Unless we confront that fact personally as well as publicly, we may find ourselves trapped in a future all of us will hate.

—A.T.

■ Let's start this on a more personal note. Many of your readers regard you as sympathetic to feminism. Are they right?

□ With respect to sexism, I can hardly remember a time in my own growing up when I did not believe that women were equal to men in all the things that matter today—brains, courage, drive, humor, creativity, responsibility and perseverance, not to mention the supposedly "feminine" traits of warmth, empathy, and willingness to share and nurture.

Over the years I have differed with organized feminism over this demand or that tactic, but the general struggle for women's rights has always seemed to me to be a good fight—a pressure in the direction of a more decent and humane future for both sexes, since restrictions on women have always entailed a corresponding, though perhaps less obvious, set of restrictions on men as well.

The painful question is why a fight should even be necessary—why women in virtually every culture have been dominated, violated, restricted, restrained, or, at best, subtly controlled by men. Of course, one can always point to specific exceptions. But the general historical pattern over literally thousands of years is beyond dispute. Why should this be so?

I, for one, have never been willing to shut off debate by simply attributing patriarchy—male domination—to God or to genes.

■ We live in a culture in which male domination, in one form or another, has been the norm. Most little boys absorb notions of male superiority in childhood. Your attitudes are not typical. Where did your own attitudes come from?

□ My own attitudes were no doubt shaped by personal experience with four remarkable women. During my early childhood, we lived together in an extended household—my grandparents, my parents, and my uncle and aunt.

My grandmother lived till nearly 90 and was strong enough and tough enough to have survived anywhere—in a pioneer hut in the American West, in a Polish shtetl, in the Arctic or in the steamy jungles of the Amazon. She had grit. My mother was, and still is, gentle and diffident, but is so thoughtful and intellectually curious that, despite never having completed her high school education, she can occasionally be found reading Kant or Hume or Bishop Berkeley. And my aunt helped bring Bohemian values and a love of poetry into my life.

Since then the woman I've observed most closely and learned the most from is my wife—my partner, my editor, my colleague, companion and critic. She is one of the most brilliant and versatile people I know. She can unscramble a medical text on neuromuscular disorder, fix a carburetor, make her own dresses on a sewing machine, get up on a platform to debate economics, cook an impressive meal, give a haircut, manage several homes, pick apples and understand tax law. She went to ground school with me and learned the electrical and hydraulic systems of my plane, and could discuss the advantages of color radar. She is an astonishing combination of the other three women, and I'm now having the pleasure of watching a fifth—my daughter—grow into full person-hood.

There were very strong men in my life, as well. My father and my uncle. There was nothing shy, retiring, dependent or effeminate about either of them. They were powerful role models for me, and I hung on their every word. They taught me all the "boy" things—soccer, carpentry, how to fix an electric motor, etc. They introduced me to politics, encouraged me to analyze the newspaper, and gave me much else. But we're talking about women right now, and no one is ever going to convince me that they are "inferior."

■ Yet personal experience seems hardly enough to account for your views. Plenty of other men have grown up with remarkable women—and still came out believing in the ultimate supremacy of the male, the "naturalness" of a sexual division of labor.

□ That's certainly true. But, in my case, my own observations were generalized and ideologized by the fact of World War II. Here we were, fighting a war against Nazism, which, among its other hideous cruelties, attempted to condemn women to *kinder-kuche-kirche*, and actually turned some of them into breeding machines for SS studs. My hatred of the Nazis helped me see that the mistreatment of women was related to the mistreatment of Jews, blacks and other groups in society. I don't believe that racism, sexism and religious bigotry are symmetric structures, or that we can draw simple analogies among them. But the interrelationships are worth study.

The reason these social pathologies are so hard to deal with is that they cut across all behavior and assume an infinite number of forms. In various countries we can find evidence of racism and sexism in job discrimination, in legal codes, in credit practices, in smirky jokes. We see it in the stereotyping of racial and national or ethnic groups, in the arrogance of the Russian vis-à-vis the Georgian or the Uzbek, the "gringo" toward the Spanish-American, the Anglo toward the Quebecois in Canada, the Japanese toward the Koreans, and in a thousand other patterns.

And then, cutting across all of these, are the assumptions of male superiority. Even now in China, a third of a century after the revolution, peasants are still beating up their wives for having the misfortune to bear them a daughter, instead of a son.

THE ORIGINS OF SEXISM

■ What's the source of the patriarchal system? You reject the idea that male dominance began with God or with our genes. In your view, then, where did it begin?

□ Who knows? There is a great deal of fascinating anthropological and archaeological speculation. But the ratio of fact to theory is minute.

When I say male supremacy is not genetic, I don't mean to throw biology out the door. It seems sensible to assume that, since women bore the babies, they operated under a built-in disadvantage vis-à-vis men in the earliest human societies. When we went from mere food gathering to hunting, it is reasonable to think the men could range farther,. could stay away longer, and had superior musculature, so that it was more or less natural for the men to hunt and the women to forage.

Hunting, in turn, may have promoted precisely those predatory characteristics and those skills of coercion that gave men increased social power over women.

Added to this is the idea expressed by the writer Marielouise Janssen-Jurreit that men had more reason than women to prefer large numbers of children, and that the greater the number of pregnancies, the less opportunity women had to compete for power. Both men and women needed children to help care for them when they were no longer capable of survival. Children were naturally bonded to their mothers. But if children were *only* bonded to their mothers, it would leave the old men of the tribe vulnerable. So, she says, the men go to work on the young boys to break their solidarity with the mother and to acculture them into the male world. This helps explain many of the puberty rites for males, the rites of passage, the secret rituals among the males, etc., in so many primitive communities.

But all this is sheer speculation. Janssen-Jurreit is a pleasure to read on all this because she recognizes how little is actually known. The real question is not how did patriarchy get started, but why does it survive in societies in which conditions are so different?

■ OK. We know that patriarchy and sexism existed long before the industrial revolution. Why did they survive? Why weren't they just swept away like so many other values and arrangements?

□ I think the reason sexism didn't vanish is that even in the industrial system women were still faced with certain biological disadvantages. Certainly the old culture, the old ideologies born out of 10,000 years of agriculture, still weighed heavily. But, in addition, when we shifted from field to factory, the new forms of work still depended mainly on sheer muscle-power. And even though women performed physical labor on the farms and in the mines and mills, men were still deemed more valuable for jobs dependent on brute strength.

On top of that, before the advent of canned milk and other prepared baby foods, the mother still could not range far from the infant—meaning she had to stay home or take the baby into the factory, which turned out to be inefficient, not to mention unhealthy and often dangerous.*

So even though the industrial revolution brought powerful changes in technology, culture, and other fields, it left the underlying biological unevenness. Until now, biology has been the slowest changing of the main systems that affect human life.

Still, the industrial revolution did give a totally new character to the relations between men and women.

■ In your work, you've focussed on the home as the key to many changes. In your judgment, what are the most important ways in which the home itself has changed?

□ The family in most First Wave or agricultural societies was big, with several generations working together as a production unit and living together under the same roof. The home, with its nearby fields, was the locus of work, the center of life. Home was also the school. It was the hospital. It was the place the elderly were cared for.

The industrial revolution ripped all these functions out of the household. Paid work for the marketplace was shifted into the factory and office and became the primary domain of the male. The school took over responsibility for education. The doctor and the

---

*Even later, when muscle-power became less important, the cultural bias against women in the economy continued and was justified on grounds that pregnancy and the demands of child care made women less dependable employees. Hence, lower wages and slower advancement. Employers thus had an incentive to retain the system, since it kept women available as a cheap labor reserve.

hospital took over care of the ill. The state took on responsibility for the elderly. The importance of the home was drastically diminished.

And the roles of men and women were sharply redefined. As Eli Zaretski has pointed out, the man moved out into a world of interdependent work and brought home the money. The woman stayed in the home and performed the older form of production—unpaid, not very interdependent, private rather than public.

■ But if the industrial revolution left the old patriarchal values in place, it might be said that these are even more structurally embedded than the technological and economic revolutions you focus on. Perhaps some of the causality runs in the other direction?

□ Some social processes are so closely linked in dense feedback relationships to one another that it is hard to separate cause from effect. They appear to be (and maybe are) simultaneously acting on each other. Certainly the two dynamics are related, and some people even argue that patriarchal attitudes were a necessary precondition for the industrial revolution. They see the whole thing as an expression of male aggression against nature, as a kind of thrusting, an almost sexual attack on the environment. I'm not over-impressed with that view, however.

What is clear is that the culture of sexism, as elaborated and updated, was spread by the mass media. It was used to justify the disadvantages faced by women, to keep them living in a closed, privatized world, and to condition them to accept and even cherish the limitations placed on them.

Even women who did enter the paid economy were channelled into low-pay low-authority jobs. Women who stayed home were praised for their "womanly" virtues, but regarded as essentially non-productive, even parasitical, despite the fact that child-rearing and housework were indirectly critical to production. Their status was low, as measured by the small number of women who held high positions in industry, government, the media or the church.

And this was still the situation when the modern women's movement began in the mid-60s, with the publication of Betty Friedan's book, *The Feminine Mystique*.

FEMINISM ON THE AGENDA

■ Betty Friedan's book was certainly not the first to challenge male supremacy.

□ No, of course not. But it was a milestone. There is, of course, a long and proud literature of feminism going back for centuries. But even within my own memory—Elizabeth Hawes wrote a book in 1948 called *Anything But Love*. In it she attacked sexism in U.S. women's magazines. I read that in 1953 in preparation for a biography I hoped to write about Lydia Maria Child, a forgotten abolitionist, feminist, and author. Child was an amazing woman who authored the first anti-slavery book in the United States, and I still have my notes. But feminism just wasn't on the agenda in the U.S. or Europe in 1952.

Even when Simone de Beauvoir's *The Second Sex* was published in the U.S. in 1953—clearly a major work on the subject—nothing happened. No movement, no protest, no action.

So I have to ask myself why did *The Feminine Mystique* explode on the American scene and suddenly help spark a new feminist movement? What happened between, say, de Beauvoir in 1953 and Friedan in 1964?

■ What were the new conditions, in your opinion?

□ One, of course, was Betty Friedan herself. I should explain that my wife, Heidi, and I have both known Betty for more than 20 years, from before *The Feminine Mystique*. That book crystallized the new mood among women, helped explain it, and put it in a conceptual framework.

Betty, herself, is one of the great organizers, one of the key social activizers in her moment of history. She actually started the National Organization for Women in her own living room. So, in addition to her ability to write, her energy and drive and tactical skill had a lot to do with starting the modern movement, which later, like all successful movements, spread out, took new forms, many of them unforeseen in the beginning.

But there were also important changes in the external conditions. Heidi has always argued that a key factor was the presence by 1964 of a whole generation of college-educated women in their thirties or older, who formed an important part of the movement, mothers whose children had already grown up and entered school. They were too smart and too energetic and too antsy just to want to stay home knitting doilies.

These women believed they were the equals of men, they had been educated to believe they could combine a career with motherhood. Then when their children were grown and they tried to enter or re-enter the job market, or even go back to college for additional training, they suddenly found the welcome mat was missing. They felt they had been lied to, cheated, misused, and they faced long empty years at home, with no "productive" role open to them. They became critical to the new feminism. And all that happened at a particular moment in the development of the U.S. economy.

During the Great Depression of the thirties, millions of women had been pushed out of the labor market. Men were typically given priority for jobs. During World War II, with so many men gone, however, the system needed workers, so Rosie the Riveter appeared. Women formed the reserve labor force. Then, after the war, the men came back and the women were expected to trot back to the kitchen again. In the early fifties, there was a real fear of unemployment. Suddenly, all the women's magazines began playing up "togetherness"—the home—the virtues of non-employment for women. The reserve army was no longer needed.

By the mid-sixties, the economy in the U.S. was booming again—it needed workers. When you put that together with the large number of educated women, some of whom faced the "empty nest syndrome," the moment was right for a revived women's movement. But this movement went far beyond jobs and economics. It soon began attacking the underlying role structure of the society as a whole.

WOMEN AND THE END OF INDUSTRIALISM

■ How does all this fit in with your thesis about the decline of industrialism and the rise of a new kind of society?

□ I would argue that some other very important things happened in precisely the years bracketed by *The Second Sex* and *The Feminine Mystique.*

In fact, what happened was that traditional industrialism reached its peak in the United States. The Second Wave was at its absolute crest, and the Third Wave of change began. Right in that decade.

For example, 1956 was the first year in which white collar and service workers outnumbered blue collar workers in the U.S. economy. We began shifting more and more out of manufacture.

Those same years saw the earliest commercial uses of the computer...the death of major mass circulation magazines and the increase in special interest publishing...the introduction of commercial jet aviation...the peak of the post-war anti-colonial movements around the world...and the introduction of the birth control pill...Sputnik....

It was a decade that ended with the riots at Berkeley and the assassination of John Kennedy.

The general crisis of industrial society was beginning —a crisis which, among other things, has seen all the old role structures of industrialism questioned and challenged: the roles of teachers and students, doctors and patients, policemen and lawyers...and most important, the roles of men and women. The political scientist Chalmers Johnson has suggested that when you want to see a real revolution, don't look at who is capturing the palace or the radio station; look at whether role structures are being transformed.

So I see the modern women's movement as engaged in a struggle to change the role definitions laid into place by the industrial revolution, and, in that sense, it is part of the large historical movement carrying us beyond traditional industrialism.

Like all social movements, it has had its share of loonies, its tactical failures, its extreme and ill-considered demands, its confusions. Like all social movements, it must enter a new stage or decay.

But, like the civil rights movement, the student movement, the anti-colonial and other movements that developed in that period, it was part of a massive critique of the world produced by the industrial revolution. It helped clarify our social problems and began to point the way to an alternate society.

A DIVERSITY OF ROLES

■ What, then, is the future of male-female relations? Will the new Third Wave civilization simply retain patriarchal relationships, as the Second Wave industrial civilization did when it replaced First Wave agriculture?

□ The question has to be put a different way because there is not likely to be a single model—a uniform system. If I am right that the entire social order is fracturing and reforming along new, more differentiated lines, then it seems unlikely to me that we will see any single dominant pattern of woman-man relationships. What we are more likely to see are a kaleidoscopic variety of role arrangements— many different communities, each with its own values and unique role structures.

Instead of a country in which everyone is more or less dragooned into becoming a member of a nuclear family—and a culture in which words like "spinster" or "bachelor" have negative connotations, or in which childlessness is seen as a reflection of "barrenness" or "sterility"—I see us moving into a period in which many different family structures crop up, flourish, and are accepted. Whether it is the electronic cottage, with mom and pop and junior working together, or it is a two-career household, or a single parent, or a lesbian pair raising a child, or a commune, or any number of other forms, there will be people living in them, and that suggests a much wider variety of male-female relationships than exists today.

■ I'm a little surprised. As the Third Wave is characterized by diversity, participation, initiative, etc., I expected you to say patriarchy would be out of sync in a Third Wave future. It seems you're saying this diversity includes even sexist forms.

☐ I can imagine the survival of communities explicitly committed to patriarchal values—Mormon communities, for example, and other traditionalist religious communities. I don't for a moment assume they are going to disappear. But I also think we are going to see communities in which the relations between the sexes would horrify traditionalists. If the theory of de-massification is right, we are unlikely to see a single dominant pattern.

However, despite the set-backs we are seeing today in the scramble for jobs, with governments that are hostile to women's rights, with the women's movement currently disheveled and uncertain about its next steps—despite all this, there are reasons for long-term optimism.

First, we are now decisively shifting away from an economy based on muscle-power to one heavily based on mind-power—and that eliminates a crucial disadvantage for women.

Next, it is possible for women to exercise far more control over birth—the timing and number of pregnancies—than ever before in history.

In addition, we're beginning to restore functions to the home, so that even women who are compelled to stay at home or consciously wish to stay at home can still, if they wish, participate directly in the exchange economy by working at home.

Then, too, the younger generation of women in the West, at least, even the most conservative among them, take for granted a range of role options their mothers and grandmothers never had. They are more independent.

And that has its reflection among young men—at least some of whom rebel against the old sex roles that gave the man dominance, but relegated him to the role of wage earner and robbed him of much of the emotional pleasure of bringing up children. So we now see young men actively caring for their infants and small children. Some even do so on a full-time basis to enable a spouse to hold on to a lucrative job or to enter a profession.

One swallow hardly makes a summer, but not long ago I saw a young couple at a table near us in a restaurant. Throughout the entire meal, the man wore an infant slung on his chest. The baby almost looked as though it were suckling. The young mother sat alongside. The idea that "parenting" is a shared responsibility— and a shared pleasure—is spreading. I know, for instance, that this idea is beginning to take root even in Japan. My publisher there asked me if I could recommend any books for translation there— books not on mothering or fathering, but on parenting.

■ Are you suggesting that even Japan, where male domination is so pronounced, will change its ways?

☐ The Japanese division of male-female roles and responsibilities is widely misunderstood in the West. We tend to think of male dominance and female submission. But that's only half the story. The Japanese male may seem all-powerful, but it's only in his own sphere. The woman may be largely confined to the home. But in the home her authority is generally supreme and unchallengeable. Typically, she gets the pay check and decides what to do with it. She usually makes all the decisions about schooling the children.

Nor is it true that there are no Japanese women in important positions. The person who initiated the television production of *The Third Wave*, conducted the key negotiations, and coordinated the project, was Chizuko Kobayashi, a woman high up on the international relations staff of NHK*. She is a delightful person with a keen sense of humor and a mind like a computer. She won her job with NHK many years ago on the strength of a competitive exam in which she outscored most of the men.

One of Japan's most important journalists is a friend of ours named Mitsuko Shimomura, who recently won something approximately like our Pulitzer Prize. She and Kobayashi-san are part of a small class of women who have "made it"—but to accomplish that they not only had to be super-women, they had to have remarkably accommodating husbands. We even know some educated Japanese women, wives of top executives, who are working at jobs over their husbands' objections.

*The Japan Broadcasting Corporation.

There is a superficial deference by women to men—outside the home. But not necessarily inside. For example, I'm just reading *Bonchi*, a novel by Toyoko Yamasaki, which centers on a shop in the merchant district in Osaka at the turn-of-the-century. For generations women have run the shop, married their own chief clerks, and subsequently dominated their lives. The themes of sex and class are intertwined. The hero runs the business successfully and chases after one mistress after another, but his private life is totally dominated by his mother and grandmother who manipulate his marriage, destroy it, and control his most personal affairs. To the outside world, he is the *bonchi* or boss. Inside, he is the victim of a matriarchy.

Whatever the Japanese male may gain by domination in one sphere may be lost by his lack of freedom in the other. Of course, this is a generalization. Many new family arrangements are springing up in Japan as in other countries. But the contrasts and division of labor are more pronounced. And the system is far too rigid. In purely economic terms, Japan is wasting a powerful asset. Japan knows that to succeed in the Third Wave it will have to be more creative than in the past. It will have to draw on the potential of its women in the economy. It will have to let hundreds of thousands of Kobayashis and Shimomuras blossom.

I think the present structure of family life in Japan is one of the things that will be hardest hit by the Third Wave. Too many Japanese still think they can advance to the new society by strategic economic and technological planning—that they can revolutionize their technology, energy, and industrial base without also substantially altering their family life and social systems.

I don't. A revolution in roles is part of the Third Wave.

So I would sum up my views this way: Although I don't expect the Third Wave to sweep away all vestiges of sexism, and to eliminate in a few decades cultural traits that have survived for millennia; and although I can see pockets of patriarchy enduring in the high tech societies for a long time—even so, I believe the basic thrust of change now favors a greater equality of the sexes. Both men and women have changed. New values are emerging, along with new technologies and economic arrangements. I may be too optimistic. But I believe that now, for the first time, a civilization is on the horizon which works for, rather than against, the historic liberation of women.

7 RACE, POWER AND CULTURE

Whose future is it anyhow?

As we suddenly confront a world of computers and satellites and video imagery, as familiar industries decline and strange new ones arise, as neighborhoods, businesses and family lives are transformed, painful political questions become inescapable.

Every civilization has its own characteristic distribution of power as between classes, sexes, races and even regions. Today as industrial civilization passes into history, powerful voices demand to know whether the emergent civilization will find room in it for the millions, indeed, billions on the earth who today are discriminated against, harassed or oppressed because of their racial, ethnic, national or religious backgrounds. Are the poor and powerless of the past going to stay that way, viewing the future, as it were, through bullet-proof glass—or will they be welcome in the new civilization we are creating?

Tough questions. And perhaps the most dangerous of all.

—A.T.

■ Will the new civilization you envision bring an end to white domination of the planet, or will it essentially be a white monopoly, perhaps with a seat at the head table reserved for the Japanese? Where do other races fit into the future? That, put bluntly, is the question we need to confront next.

□ Anyone who thinks that power and economic wealth in the future will be monopolized by the white race, with or without the Japanese, is in for a big jolt.

But first, some definitions. In everyday terms, people still tend to think of the world as chiefly made up of whites, blacks, yellows and browns—as though race were mainly a matter of color and a handful of categories were enough to exhaust the range of human possibility. Actually, a race can better be described as a population in which some cluster of biological characteristics appears with greater frequency than it does outside the group...skin color, bone structure or hair texture, for example. But it all depends on what you're looking for and what criteria you apply. One scientist has classified humans into nine different races—and still found 32 groups that wouldn't fit neatly into the scheme. Another classification provides for up to 200 categories. And I suspect that as our knowledge of genetics advances, we will differentiate even more, and on the basis of quite invisible traits like susceptibility to this or that disease, as we already do with sickle cell anemia.

But what we think of as "racial" is often social or cultural, and, as you know, even terms like "ethnic group," "religion," and "nationality" are all fuzzy...

THE WHITE INTERLUDE

■ Of course there are serious problems of definition. I doubt, for example, that there is any solid biological basis for racial distinctions, and think, instead, that racial boundaries as we know them are socially fixed. But either way, or in whatever combination, we know broadly what we mean by "race." And I think the essential question is very clear in everyday terms. Is the future you project going to be white-dominated—and, if not, why not?

□ I don't think there can be too much argument about the fact that the world today is still basically white-dominated. The super-powers, the economic giants are mainly in the Northern hemisphere and mainly populated or ruled by whites. And some people no doubt think that is the natural condition of life.

Yet white control over large parts of the earth is a recent historical development. It began some 300-400 years ago, and it is now in decline. Our descendants, glancing back from a thousand years hence, may regard the last few hundred years as the "white interlude."

This period began when the Europeans moved out of their own continent. When they discovered the New World, they promptly subjugated the Indians and took over both North and South America. When they discovered the trade route to India, they outflanked Islam, which basically dominated the Mediterranean, and proceeded to colonize Asia and Africa. They expanded the trade in black slaves. Later, as European industrialization picked up steam, so did the push for colonies, and the Europeans managed to establish a chain of "feeder" societies that pumped cheap food, energy and raw materials into their expanding economies. This is, of course, a gross description, but in *The Third Wave* I've discussed the process in detail and with appropriate qualifications, pointing out the ways in which imperialism served the needs of both capitalist and "socialist" industrial nations.

In any case, this roll of the Second Wave across the earth was part of the expansion of industrialism. But what it also meant was the conquest of the non-white world.

The first setback to this great white advance—an event crucial to world racial history, yet almost totally ignored in American schoolbooks—was the military defeat of the Russians by the Japanese in 1904. It was the first time in centuries that a major European power was stopped cold by a non-white nation, and it sent a thrill of racial pride throughout Asia. Chinese intellectuals wrote poems about it.

Was this Japanese success primarily a matter of race? Or was it smokestacks and machine guns? For Japan by now was on its way to becoming a Second Wave, industrial power. And before long it began playing the Second Wave imperialist game itself—only with a twist. As its troops grabbed up new markets and raw materials in China, Korea, and elsewhere, they announced they were doing so to protect these countries from white imperialism! Japan even continued to use that line during World War II.

■ You're laying heavy stress on economic as against cultural considerations. Are you implying that racial issues are of less importance?

□ Not at all. I don't mean to imply that race is necessarily subordinate to plain old economic smash-and-grab—though it sometimes is. I'm fully aware that imperialism was not just a matter of economics, but was also very often the imposition of religion, culture, and a sense of inferiority on the colonized populations. I would never underestimate the importance of racial feelings in today's world, especially after they have been rubbed raw by a few centuries of largely white imperialism.

■ But you say that interlude is now reaching an end. You more or less correlate the beginning of the "white interlude" with the coming of industrialism. Are you suggesting that the coming of the Third Wave marks the beginning of the end of the interlude?

□ I'm not suggesting causation. But it is worth noting that the decade 1955-65, when the Third Wave was beginning in the United States, was also the high point of de-colonization around the world. It was in that decade that many of the former colonies gained political independence. And since then we have seen rising militancy and racial pride on the part of literally billions of people around the world who were previously subordinated to European, American, Soviet—or Japanese—power.

The manifestations of that wounded pride are myriad. They range from violence right on down to language. Recently, for example, the People's Republic of Mongolia protested the use of the term "mongol" to describe sufferers from the disease known as Down's Syndrome. The Mongolians are fully aware, as most of the rest of us have not been, that the term originated precisely as a racial slur. (Dr. Down in the 1860s referred to the disease's victims as "Mongolian idiots" on grounds that their illness was somehow a throwback to an "inferior race.")

There has also been a shift in the racial distribution of world power. The spectacular rise of Arab financial and political potency in the 1970s and early 1980s may have already topped out. Weaknesses in O.P.E.C. and misdirected development strategies may combine to reduce that suddenly accrued power. But it is unlikely we will ever go back to the *status quo ante*. Arab representatives are now and will remain part of the world power structure.

Now add to that the dramatic upsurge of Japan, Taiwan, Hong Kong, Singapore and South Korea in recent years and the extremely rapid economic growth rate in much of the East Asian and Pacific Region. This new historical fact suggests that the Asian and Pacific peoples are also before long going to be sharing world influence with the U.S., the Soviets and the Europeans.

As computers proliferate in Asia, as the Chinese (and the Overseas Chinese) develop their own word-processing systems capable of handling their ideographic language, as satellites beam data back and forth over formerly isolated regions of the Pacific, as Ph.D.s in India or Singapore write software for computers in Manhattan or Minneapolis, we are also likely to see a powerful flow of financial, cultural and other influences from East to West.

Right now many "developing countries" fear the spread of computing will Westernize their cultures. But quite the reverse is also conceivable—that the very way we think, design computers or software, may itself take on a different character as non-Western cultures enter the field.

While the outcomes are by no means clear, the fact of change is undeniable. The centers of world economic and cultural influence are on the move. Banking is no longer so heavily concentrated in

London, New York or Zurich. Mexico City, today, despite being a polluted sink-hole of overurbanization, is more intellectually alive than half a dozen European capitals. It is churning with artists, political refugees, intellectuals. And perhaps the best fiction in the world is coming out of South America.

Two other, more material factors are also likely to accelerate the dispersal of world power. One is the changed distribution of arms around the world. We needn't go into the reasons or dangers here. But the realistic fact is that now even quite small states can have highly lethal weaponry at their command, which means they can "talk back" to a degree never before possible during the (not entirely) white interlude. For good or ill, that also begins to change the world power balance.

And finally, a key, almost totally overlooked point. Resources. The present system, still based on the needs of Second Wave mass production, relies on a handful of resources used in vast quantities. As Third Wave de-massified manufacturing methods spread, and production itself is decentralized, we are going to use different, more diverse resources, probably in smaller quantities. This means a further radical redistribution of economic power on the earth.

So that at many different levels simultaneously we're seeing an historic redistribution of influence and authority on the planet. Admittedly, some of this is pure speculation. But, no. In answer to your original question, I do not think that the rest of the planet is going to be excluded from Third Wave civilization or that the future belongs to any one race. In long-range, historical terms, I think the white interlude is going to be replaced by a "technicolor" future.

■ In all this, you haven't said a single word about Africa. Why?

☐ Because I know the least about it. Again, I am only speculating, but it seems to me that Africa faces the most difficult hurdles of all, partly because of the insane political patterns imposed on it by the Second Wave imperial powers—pseudo-nation-states superimposed on tribal arrangments; pseudo-parliaments; pseudo-Oxfords and Sorbonnes. With the festering racist sore at its southern tip and its tremendous strategic significance, it is a prime playground for super-power games and proxy wars, from Angola to the Horn. And it has all its own internal problems like unbridled corruption, the brutality of many of its regimes, not to mention inter-tribal warfare.

■ You picture a seething world of change in which, somehow, the central power of the super-states, the U.S. and the U.S.S.R., is reduced and the power of the oppressed people grows...

☐ I wouldn't put it that way. Oppression is another matter, and it's obvious that millions of ex-colonial people are now brutally oppressed by their own rulers. Oppression is a separate question. The issue I am addressing is whether the present crude imbalance of world power is stable. Can we shift out of the industrial age toward a new Third Wave civilization and expect the same distribution of power between regions and races?

No.

THE TECHNICOLOR PROBLEM

■ Doesn't what you call a "technicolor" distribution of power pose special problems for the United States? Not just economic problems, but cultural ones as well? Can Americans, steeped in racist traditions and accustomed to super-power status, get used to power-sharing in a Third Wave world, when they don't seem to be able to accept power-sharing with racial and ethnic minorities at home?

☐ Americans—and Soviets, too—will have to get used to the new distribution of world power in the next two or three decades, just as Britain and France have had to get used to the loss of empire. This may come as a psychological and cultural blow, not to speak of economics, especially since cultural arrogance and a certain provincialism are still part of the American make-up. But it is worth reminding ourselves that the mistreatment of racial, religious and ethnic minorities is hardly a Yankee invention.

Rotten as the American record may be, it isn't so different from that in other nations—and, in some respects, it is better. Americans, at least, have done a lot of public soul-searching over this question. The country has lived through the experience of the melting pot, the civil rights crusades, the flames in Bedford-Stuyvesant and Watts. And, as poorly enforced as they are, there now are laws and court decisions on the books that work in favor of ethnic and racial equality of opportunity. That's not necessarily true in other countries, a lot of which won't even admit that they have a problem.

When the riots were blazing in Harlem and Watts and other black communities in the 1960s, I can remember the British media taking a certain malicious delight in America's misfortunes, as though racism could never rear its ugly head in a traditionally tolerant Britain.

Unfortunately, gang attacks on or by young Pakistanis and West Indians are now a regular occurrence in London and elsewhere. Unemployment rates are skewed against minorities in Britain, too,* and you see racist graffiti on tube stations and public buildings.

Call it racism, call it persecution of minorities, but in Paris the hatred for Algerian migrant workers is overt. In 1981 the Communist Party appealed to anti-black and anti-Arab sentiments to win votes. Georges Marchais, the French C.P. candidate, told an audience he didn't want "new Harlems or new Sowetos in the Paris suburbs." And there are new fascist movements in France, on both the so-called left and the right, that are fiercely anti-black, anti-Arab, anti-semitic. The CGT, the main French labor federation, in fact, has attacked another union for allegedly being "zionist," and the recent bombings of synagogues in Paris, whether by Arabs or by French anti-semites, and the French government's fumbling and insensitive responses all call to mind the sickness of the pre-war era.

---

*Each country defines "white" and "non-white" in different ways. The British census does not ask racial questions directly, but responsible estimates put the number of non-whites in Britain at approximately 4,000,000. Between 1972-81 overall unemployment rose 138 percent. Among non-whites it rose 325 percent.

In Germany, meanwhile, hatred for the underclass of Turkish immigrants is so rabid, that even the Social Democratic politicians appeal to it. Helmut Schmidt himself has made jibes at the "smell of garlic" among Turks, which is about like making watermelon jokes in the U.S.

Ask the Japanese, and mostly they'll tell you they are fortunate not to have a "race problem." But ask the Koreans who live in Japan and they'll tell a different story.

I say all this not to whitewash the situation in the U.S., but to make the point that racism—and I now use the term simply to mean the oppression of minorities and alternative cultures in the most general sense—racism is extremely widespread and has very deep roots.

It isn't a Yankee plot or a capitalist phenomenon, as the Russians would have us believe. In fact, I witnessed a classic bit of white racism one night in Moscow.

■ When was that?

□ In 1976. We were there as guests of the American embassy. We spent an evening with two young Africans. One was studying engineering in Moscow. The other had already graduated from a Moscow academy. Having lived there for years, they both hated Moscow bitterly, and spoke about the blatant racism there.

Together we went up to a hotel clerk to ask directions to a certain restaurant. Since the two Africans spoke fluent Russian, and Heidi and I spoke none, one of them spoke directly to the clerk in her own language. The clerk, looking through him as though he were Ralph Ellison's "invisible man," gave the directions to us, instead, in broken, barely comprehensible English. The two Africans simply didn't exist for her.

But, then again, neither do some of the non-Russian minorities within the Soviet Union. Soviet anti-semitic persecution is known all over the world. But many Russians also hold nastily racist attitudes toward Moslems and other minorities. And in Moscow we were repeatedly warned by Russians against the so-called "yellow peril" posed by China.

The Soviets are a nation of many nations, but there is little doubt about who is in charge. For example, there are reports of outbreaks of racial and ethnic violence in the Red Army, in which the officers tend to be Russian, the non-coms Ukrainian, and the troops made up largely of other nationalities or racial groups. Racist Russians call their Central Asian people "churkas"—which means dumb or worthless, blockheads, in effect. In turn the Balts call the Russians "cukes"—which means swine.

Meanwhile, Czechoslavakia, another "worker's paradise," is importing cheap labor from Vietnam and Cuba. It is reportedly about to receive a large contingent from Mozambique. Recently the Vietnamese in Prague experienced first-hand the same kind of treatment that a Turk in Germany or an American black would find familiar. Local toughs tried to burn down their hostel and threw stones at them. When the Vietnamese fought back on another night, the police showed precisely where their sympathies lay. In another incident, Czech workers in a shoe factory demanded a No Viet employment policy.

And here, precisely as in South Boston or Liverpool, the issues of race and class become inextricably intertwined. The Vietnamese workers in the building industry, for example, are paid less than a third of the wages Czech workers get. When the Vietnamese went on strike for higher wages (!), the authorities simply shut off the electricity to their hostel.

There is speculation in the European press that these Vietnamese laborers are Vietnam's way of paying off its war debt to the Czechs. The Vietnamese work for a fraction of the normal wages, and the Czech government pockets the differential.

Alas, this litany could go on and on. I'll just add one more thought.

Individual communists in many countries often fought courageously against racism and consciously attempted to root racist attitudes out of their psyches. Some have even given their lives. But Marxism, itself, despite its egalitarian rhetoric, regards racial injustice as a side-issue—like sexism. The argument is that equality is impossible until the class struggle is won. So feminists, and blacks, Latins or Asians fighting racism have been repeatedly asked to postpone or subordinate their goals to those of the working class—meaning, as a rule, the male, mainstream workers. It's a point that hasn't been lost on Third World people.

And while we're onto that, the so-called Third World hasn't much to brag about either. I would hate to be a dark-skinned non-Muslim in the Sudan, or on the losing end of the conflict between black Fijians and East Indians in Fiji, Chinese and Malays in Malaysia, etc., etc.

All in all, it's a pathetic picture. Against all that, I would not rate the American performance at either the top or the bottom of the list. Regrettably, xenophobia thrives!

LAYERS OF IDENTITY

■ In your work you've presented an overview in which you've tried to take account of many factors usually ignored in social analysis. But, as with the case of sexism, here again we are up against a set of attitudes and social relations that have persisted through all the technoeconomic waves of change. How do you relate these to your theories of change?

□ To me racial, ethnic, religious and other forms of discrimination are all ultimately rooted in the evolutionary need of the individual for some form of group identification. Groups that managed to create a degree of cohesiveness probably survived better than those that didn't. All societies have what I call a "psycho-sphere" which encompasses their ideas of community and identity. So the idea of "belonging" or "community" and the act of identifying with others is a fundamental part of the glue of all human social systems.

But I don't believe any of this overrides the waves of change I have discussed. For with each historic wave of change we have seen revolutionary changes in the nature of individual and group identity.

For example, during the 10,000 years of agricultural dominance on the planet, the period of First Wave civilization, individuals identified most strongly with family, clan, village, religion, or other groupings that, for all practical purposes, captured the individual at birth. You were born into a family and a racial group. You lived out your entire life in the village of birth. Your religion was given you by your parents and the local community and seldom, if ever, challenged during your life-time. So the most basic of individual and group allegiances were determined at birth. The individual had little or no choice in the matter, and the group identity usually remained permanent throughout one's life.

When the industrial revolution sent the Second Wave of change across the earth, the need for belonging remained, but the nature of individual and group affiliation changed markedly. Now, instead of your village, you were encouraged to identify with your nation. Class consciousness provided another form of identification and belonging. The division of labor produced entirely new groupings.

In fact, the Second Wave of change introduced a new "layer" of identity, as it were.

While many of the older identifications remained, they were integrated with a new layer of what might be called identifying features. Some of the older identifications lost their emotional force as new ones gained.

As the Second Wave stripped away functions of the family, for instance, family ties were weakened—as reflected in the fact that responsibility for the elderly was transferred from their children to the state. National allegiance grew stronger, local bonds weaker. And so on. But, once more, the dominant identifications, apart from occupational ties, were still either fixed or heavily influenced at birth.

Now the Third Wave arrives and it, too, will change the nature of identity. I believe it will do this in two basic ways.

First, if I am right about the shift toward a more heterogenous, more differentiated society, then we ought to expect to see a far greater variety of identifications and groupings. And that is precisely what is happening.

Not only is the body politic in the U.S. and other high technology nations breaking into more segments, and the consumer market reflecting more diverse individual and group needs, and more subcultures breaking away from the dominant values of the majority, but the same centrifugal processes are at work *within* minority groups themselves.

Racial, ethnic and religious sub-groups in each society are themselves segmenting into smaller, more self-defining, more varied mini-groups. It is simply no longer appropriate to speak of American blacks as a homogenous group or to lump Hispanics together.

In fact, the very notion of what constitutes a politically relevant minority is changing. Differences that once seemed trivial are taking on cultural and political significance, and it is not accidental that we are beginning to see militant organizing now on the part of such groups as the elderly, the physically handicapped, homosexuals, and others who believe they are mistreated by the mass society. New identity-groups emerge, and this yeasty, bubbling social process will be decidedly accelerated by the de-massified media—special interest publications, cable television, direct broadcast satellites, videocassettes, and the like.

Moreover, the individual is less and less bound by birth and has greater choice of self-definition. Of course, we are all still born into families, racial groups, and so forth. But it is clearly the case that as the Third Wave advances many people gain increased choice, corresponding with the increase in individuality and heterogeneity in the new social structure.

Furthermore, the coming of the Third Wave is also associated with a marked acceleration in rates of social and cultural change, so that the identifications people choose tend to be more transitory as well, with people adopting and shedding parts of their identities at a more rapid rate than ever.

These are overlaid on the older, presumably more deeply-embedded layers of racial and ethnic identity.

For all these reasons, therefore, I think it fair to say that the arrival of the Third Wave *does* qualitatively change even this oldest of human problems—identity.

THE PRIMACY OF CULTURE

■ But let's get back from theory to reality.

□ Good.

■ Despite the changes you describe, the power of racism, in the broadest sense, seems undiminished, and as your new economy emerges, won't minorities have an even harder time gaining access to decent jobs? Don't we face more of a risk of increasing the size of the underclass that already exists in all the high technology countries? Returning to the United States, for example, given the unequal access to income and knowledge that prevails, isn't it going to be harder for a young black or Hispanic to find a job if the U.S. economy continues to move relentlessly toward computers, electronics and other Third Wave industries?

□ It's a question of social policy, not technology. I don't have any magic cure for unemployment or. for racial and ethnic discrimination. And I'm certainly not pollyannish about the life-chances of minority youth. But nothing stands still, and the present political lull is not likely to last. And it all depends on what we do about it.

If we allow the full burden of structural changes in the economy to fall onto the backs of those least prepared to deal with it, we may well force the issues out of Congress or the courts and into the streets.

Present government policies, even on the so-called "left," in my opinion dramatically underestimate this danger. We are, bit by bit, building up the odds for outbreaks of civil disorder and a level of political instability that cannot be sustained for long. People will, after all, fight back when their backs are driven against the wall, and we live in a period when even quite small groups can be extremely disruptive once they set their minds to it.

I don't anticipate a simple repetition of, say, the late 1960s, when the ghettos were on fire. I don't think we're going to relive the past.

But if conditions become desperate, the reactions could actually be worse. I can imagine spontaneous outbreaks of violence and carefully organized terrorism, along with all sorts of other horrors. And if angry blacks do burn anything down, it will probably no longer be confined to their own neighborhoods. Moreover, the "fire next time" may not be black in origin. Other groups have equally deep and frustrating grievances, not to mention the poor and unemployed of the majority populations.

Look. The Second Wave is waning and the jobs based on it are drying up or relocating in cheap-labor countries. The Third Wave is on the rise and new jobs are opening up. How many of these there will be depends on how intelligently governments and businesses plan the transition.

If they are stupid about it there could be plenty of trouble, including anarchic violence.

Right now, despite high unemployment, the streets are still relatively peaceful—so far as protest goes. That's because unemployment today is simply not the same as it was a generation ago. There is at least some minimal support structure in place for a good many of the unemployed. There are a great many two-job or even two-career families. There is a degree of job sharing and an increasing amount of part-time work. And the conditions are still very spotty, so that London cabbies tell you they are having a terrific season—while auto workers outside London walk the streets. Detroit hurts a lot. Dallas only a little.

But if things were to go very bad, political stability could vanish overnight and even the most benighted, neanderthal politician or baron of business senses this. The prevailing mood among the top people in all these countries isn't "Terrific, we've got the bloody workers on the run!" so much as it is fear, malaise, and upset about the difficulties in their own particular industries. What they are worried about, however, is some sort of replay of the 1930s. They don't yet recognize that everything is different, so that even the forms of protest are likely to be more demassified, decentralized, hard to predict and even harder to suppress.

My advice would be: pay special attention to minorities—all sorts of minorities and even mini-minorities. That's where the greatest pain is at the moment, and it is also where the greatest potential for conflict lies.

■ And what advice would you have for leaders of these minorities and mini-minorities? What strategies should they be using, in your opinion?

☐ The key failure, I think, of minority group leadership today is the mirror, the flip-side of the failure of our top business and government leadership: The failure to look ahead.

If I were advising some hard-pressed minority group, I would first say, "Look, I don't have the answers. You're going to have to solve your own problems. No one is going to do it for you. And it's very easy to talk—or write, especially when your belly is full. It's hard to do all the things necessary when you have no resources."

But I would also suggest that old strategies, old policies, old approaches, won't work any longer. And that unless new policies are based on the future, rather than the past, they are a dead end.*

Strategies based solely on the idea of hanging on to a piece of the Second Wave "action"—to jobs, for example, in the dying industries—are just not enough.

I would pay special attention to the Third Wave sector of the economy, and for a simple reason. It may actually be easier to win certain gains—training programs, for example—in the growing Third Wave sector than in the shrinking Second Wave sector of the economy. But it still makes more sense to fight for a piece of tomorrow than for a piece of yesterday.

That means carefully studying the hidden restructuring—the economic upheaval—now going on in the high technology countries: the shift to new industries like computers and communications or the latest services in fields like health or support industries like medical electronics. It means recognizing the long-

*See "Can Organized Religion Be Relevant in the New Emerging Society?" speech by Offie Wortham at the Social Change Institute on Non-Violence, at the Martin Luther King, Jr., Center, Atlanta, Georgia, July 29, 1980.

term shift toward local and regional production and the decentralization of production that is already under way. It means recognizing the implications of de-urbanization. It may—not necessarily, but may—mean going where the Third Wave jobs are; or it may mean helping to create Third Wave jobs where the unemployed already live. It means looking closely at new forms of work that can be done at home, making use of the new technologies. It means recognizing that some people, because of age, lack of confidence, personality disorders or other problems, aren't going to find places in the new sectors of industry, even if there are ten jobs open to them. Especially for such people, it means looking closely at new approaches to self-help, community development, sweat equity, etc. Recognizing that many jobs in mass manufacturing are going to disappear, and not just jobs now held by minority workers, it means literally getting together to try to *invent* new services and goods and find markets for them. It also means, obviously, putting as much political pressure as possible on the authorities—often local, state or regional, rather than merely national—for support for these policies and for the survival funds needed to see the crisis through.

Above all, however, it means that training and more training and still more training, along with education for the children, get top priority in any comprehensive program. In short, it means facing the future, not the past.

Nor is it only minorities who are in trouble as the Third Wave sweeps in. We are all confronting an essentially new culture. It's as if some invading force had arrived from elsewhere and suddenly announced that, from now on, everyone is going to have to learn to ski on one leg while thinking in Esperanto. We all have a lot of learning and adapting to do.

How many times recently have we heard a parent or grandparent marvel at his or her offspring who at seven or ten years old is busily programming a computer. The pride is almost always followed with "I'm too old for this" or "I know I'm being left behind." There is a growing popular awareness that a new culture is taking form around us. And its not just computers. It's video. It's new attitudes toward work, sex, nation, leisure, authority, etc.

In the Second Wave there was a mass culture and you were supposed to fit into it. In the Third Wave period there is no single culture, but a continually changing diversity of new cultures. That is very hard for anyone to grasp, minority group member or not.

And the more we move toward a Third Wave economy, the more culture matters. Many of the new occupations in these industries are culture-dependent in ways that were not true in the past. The new economy pays off for skills in handling symbols, images and abstractions, for the ability to speak and articulate logically, and for other abilities that, until now, have been the least necessary and the least rewarded in minority populations, many of which are still close to their pre-industrial, agricultural roots.

The old economy of the Second Wave era paid off for certain traits: punctuality; obedience to a single, central authority; understanding of how bureaucracy functioned; resignation to a lifetime of rote and repetitive toil, and so forth.

The new Third Wave economy also rewards certain traits, as I've already suggested, but they won't necessarily be the same. Clearly, it pays big rewards for cognitive skills and education. But there are many other personal skills that will be in short supply. The Third Wave economy will also reward people who are quickly adaptive to change; who are flexible, able to work for more than one boss, and maybe even, at the same time, to serve *as* a boss: It will pay off for people who are curious, inquisitive, eager to find out what is going on and to influence it; people who can keep their heads in the midst of disorder and ambiguity. It will pay for people who may not have the skills of a life-long specialist, but rather experience in several different fields and the ability to transfer ideas from one to the other. It will reward individuality and entrepreneurialism.

It will find places in it for people who are good conciliators and mediators, able to move back and forth among conflicting organizations, listening to each side in turn, and interpreting it to the other. (Like entrepreneurialism, by the way, this is a skill that we can find right now, in any ghetto or barrio, in among the street gangs.) The Third Wave economy will favor self-starters, doers, but it will also need creative dreamers in larger numbers than before. It will favor—and this is crucial—those who are future-oriented over those who live primarily in the past. And so on. No one racial or ethnic group, no religion or nationality, has a monopoly on these traits. Each culture, whether West Indian, Filipino, Algerian, Turkish, Cuban or Korean, comes to the Third Wave with its own social character developed over the centuries. Each rewarded certain of these traits and punished others. It is the match between the cultures of the past and the emerging Third Wave cultures of the future that will heavily determine how different mini-minorities fare in the new civilization—which, far more than the mass society of the past, will be a continually changing mosaic of mini-minorities.

All these skills and traits, it is true, will, for the foreseeable interim, have to be accompanied by at least some elementary skills like reading and, to a lesser degree, writing, plus some (but not necessarily a great deal) of math. Seeing the semi-literacy or actual illiteracy around us, many people wonder whether this hurdle can ever be overcome.

What most of us forget is that we are also developing new tools for delivering these skills. There are children today who are playing a form of Space Invaders, a video game in which they do not drop bombs but commas, and are rewarded if they put the commas in the right place in a sentence. This is only the first, most primitive example of a whole new class of learning tools that can, if we are sensible, provide the necessary skills to everyone. Math? Yes, it's fine to have a command of trigonometry or calculus; but for many jobs a tiny hand-held calculator with minimal functions may be all that is required.

I said a moment ago that different cultures rewarded different human traits. And today we live at a time when many minority groups are busily rediscovering their own history as part of the process of recovering a lost dignity. Oppressed groups, having been called inferior, need to transit through the past to find strength.

But we are entering a period when culture counts more than ever, and culture is not something frozen in amber; it is what we create anew each day. The Third Wave will embrace many cultures.

Frantz Fanon, the black psychiatrist, wrote a proud, powerful book that moved me, as it also stirred readers around the world. In *Black Skin White Mask*, he said: "In no way should I derive my basic purpose from the past of the peoples of colour...I will not make myself the man of any past. I do not want to exalt the past at the expense of my present and of my future."

Not just for minorities—whether the dark minorities within the high technology nations or the white minority on the planet— yesterday is not enough.

PART TWO
PREMISES

Life is the art of drawing sufficient conclusions from insufficient premises.

Note-books
Samuel Butler

Come in here! You have nothing to lose but your preconceptions!

Options
Robert Sheckley

8 PREMISSORY NOTES

Premises are starting points. Origins. Assumptions we normally take for granted.

To understand any author's ideas, it helps to know where—in the vernacular—he or she is "coming from."

With this in mind, we agreed early on that some of these talks would be devoted to my personal background, methods of work, and intellectual models. There was no intention of providing a biography—or even a sketch of one. But enough information to give some context to the ideas presented here. Similarly, we knew it is impossible for any author to surface all of his or her assumptions, even with the help of skillful prodding. Nevertheless, we felt that by examining even a few of them, we could deepen our understanding of the rest.

I acquiesced to this more personal probing, because I thought I would learn something from it also. And I did.

By now, we had spoken of politics, technology, communications, racism, sexism, economics, philosophy and family life.

Now the talks took a sharply different tack.

—A.T.

■ Who is Alvin Toffler? You are one of a small number of contemporary authors whose ideas have had a world-wide influence. Yet not much is known about you as a person. In our remaining interviews, we'd like to explore that impact and its philosophical roots. So, let's start with your own self-image. Do you think of yourself as essentially a writer, a social critic, or a futurist?

□ That's an uncomfortable question because the notion that I am an "author" or a "social critic" or a "futurist" is one-dimensional. I could also be identified as a happy husband, a proud father, a six-footer, a pilot, a son, a sibling, a movie-goer, a taxpayer, an intellectual, an American. Which facet of me does your "who" apply to? And at which particular moment?

■ Are you so different from moment to moment?

□ I once wrote about the concept of "serial selves"—and all of us, of course, transit through time. If you had asked me "who" I was 30 years ago, I would have said a welder, a foundry millwright, a punch press operator, a blacksmith's helper. But under that you would have found a university graduate, an aspiring poet and novelist, a political radical, a romantic.

■ And now? Do any of these terms still apply?

□ Naturally, I'm still a university graduate.

■ A poet?

□ I still write poetry.

■ A political radical?

□ Not in any conventional sense.

■ And are you still a romantic?

□ I've been mistakenly called a utopian. I have a touch of romanticism in me. I still can be stirred by the sight of the space shuttle and the image of the earth as seen from space. But I am too skeptical of most things to be a successful romantic.

■ One of the things that sets you apart from most intellectuals is the fact that you spent five years in blue collar work. Wasn't it an unusual leap to go from factories and foundries to being a best-selling, world-famous author?

☐ Yes, but it has a hidden logic of its own. Ever since childhood, I always wanted to write. And I've also been interested in social issues and political change since my school days. So all that was there before I ever set foot in a factory.

■ But why did you choose factory work? Most people who work in factories have few alternatives. You chose to. Why?

☐ I went out of a mixture of motives. Heidi—then my girlfriend—went with me, and we shared the experience. Part of my motivation was psychological—the normal drive of a young man to get away from his home, to experience a different world. I went to the university with thousands of ex-G.I.s. They were older than I, more mature, more sophisticated. They had seen the world from Guadalcanal to Normandy. I was six months too young to serve in World War II. I felt that going into a Midwest factory would take me out of academia and plunge me into the "real world."

I also had literary motives. Steinbeck had picked grapes. Jack London had shipped out to sea. Other authors I admired had driven trucks and done many other things. I found the thought romantic, and dreamed of writing a great novel about working class life.

Finally, I was a political activist. In the late 1940s I had travelled in the South working for civil rights. I had marched in demos and discovered Marxism, which sees the factory as the exact center of the universe. So going "into industry" also meant a chance to help organize the workers. All this was heady stuff.

■ What kinds of work did you do?

☐ Ran a punch press. Became a millwright in a steel foundry. Worked as a metal finisher on an auto assembly line. Got to do many different things, from using a jack hammer to driving a forklift. I painted stripes on bicycles, worked on cars and trucks, stamped out grilles for window fans, repaired broken conveyor lines, cleaned exhaust ducts, built dust control equipment for African mines. Heidi worked in an aluminum foundry for years and was elected a shop steward for the United Auto Workers.

I learned as much in the factory as I had in the classroom. On the one hand, I came to recognize the silliness and arrogance of left-wing intellectuals who set out to "raise the class consciousness" of American workers. On the other, I also saw first-hand the stupidities of management—the callousness that justified unsafe conditions, the deviousness and patronizing attitudes of the people in white shirts who dealt with blue collar people.

I did not discover a "noble savage" or some "glorious proletarian" under the blue denim. I don't believe in romanticizing any class. But I did find plenty of intelligence, decency and a sense of humor in most of the workers, including those trapped in dirty, monotonous, and sometimes brutal jobs.

I developed a lifelong aversion to intellectuals who have never worked a day on an assembly line or on a punch press, yet write learned disquisitions telling us that workers "don't mind" boredom because, after all, they don't know any better. Or that workers don't want responsibility.

I also learned a lot about the English language—how to write so that people without Ph.D.s can understand it. I discovered that it's a lot harder to write in popular prose than in academic jargon meant to be read only by other academics.

I might have shortened the blue-collar period in my life, and there were times I absolutely hated it. But I don't regret it at all.

WELDER AT THE WHITE HOUSE

■ How did you make the transition out of blue collar life into writing?

□ Via journalism. First by writing about welding—which I had learned to do. Later by writing about industrial relations, strikes, economics, trade union affairs, labor conditions, which, by then, I also knew something about.

The factory was my graduate school.

■ You worked for a trade journal. You became a journalist in the labor press. You free lanced for magazines, and then, in the late 1950s, became a newspaper correspondent in Washington.

☐ Yes. For three years I covered the White House and Capitol Hill for a Pennsylvania daily. I may have been the only ex-welder at the White House! That meant covering Eisenhower's presidential press conferences, along with House and Senate hearings on everything from disarmament to antitrust problems. I covered the departments—Labor, Commerce, Interior, and the agencies like the FCC and the FTC. I free lanced pieces to the *Christian Science Monitor*, the *Washington Star*, and even the foreign press. I think one of my articles on U.S. nuclear policy wound up in *Asahi Shimbun* in Tokyo. Then I left Washington to join the staff of *Fortune* magazine.

■ That must have been a big ideological leap. To go from the labor press to the leading business magazine?

☐ I became labor columnist for the magazine. My job was to interpret labor-management relations—to make sense of some of the complexities—not provide ideological ammunition for anyone. Only once did an editor try to stuff some overt anti-union propaganda into my column. It had to do with steel negotiations, as I recall. But I was able to stand my ground.

In any case, I soon began writing more general articles. I investigated a nasty conflict of interest scandal in Chrysler and studied Coca-Cola's marketing. I also suggested, and then wrote, an article on the economics of the arts in the U.S.

■ When did you first get interested in technology and its social implications?

☐ Recently I discovered an ancient copy of a college magazine I edited as a student. And there I found articles I had written that referred to technology and social change. So my interest existed very early. The labor experience sharpened it.

And in 1961, shortly after leaving *Fortune*, IBM asked me to write a white paper for them on the long-range organizational implications of the computer and white collar automation.

That was a long time ago—long before we began speaking of word processors and the so-called "office of the future." At about the same time, I also did a study of information retrieval for a foundation called the Educational Facilities Laboratories. I travelled around the country interviewing the researchers who laid the basis for today's advances in artificial intelligence.

■ What about writing?

☐ I began free-lancing again for a lot of magazines. Free-lancing is a terrific school, because you're trained to do research in many fields, to find the smartest people, to interview, to investigate, to organize your thoughts, and to set them down within the constraints of magazine form, and to do all that against a deadline. I also began work on a book.

■ *The Culture Consumers?*

☐ Yes, it came out in 1964. It was an analysis of the economics of the arts in the U.S., and an attack on cultural elitism.

■ How did you go from a book about the arts and an attack on cultural elitism to *Future Shock* six years later?

☐ *Future Shock* was actually inspired by my earlier experiences in Washington. As a correspondent, I came to the conclusion that major social and technological changes were shaking up American society, but that our government was facing backward—that it devoted little attention to the future and seemed unable to anticipate even the most fundamental changes. The politicians could seldom look beyond the next election.

That got me thinking about time and time horizons, and, more generally, about our failure to deal with change and the future...our inability to cope. Not just governments, but people.

■ How long did it take to write *Future Shock*?

☐ Five years from conception to completion. But, of course, in that same period I was still writing articles, not just for popular magazines but for journals like *Technology and Culture* and the *Annals of the American Academy of Political and Social Science*. I also began teaching a course on the sociology of the future at the New School for Social Research and I became a Visiting Professor at Cornell University, where I and another professor taught a course on the relationship of technology and values. We developed a complex simulation of the feedback between value change and technological advance.

Then, in 1970, *Future Shock* was published.

RADIOS IN THE JUNGLE

■ How did the publication of *Future Shock* change your life?

☐ In several ways. You can't have a tremendous avalanche of response such as was triggered by *Future Shock* without it having an effect on your life. The most important impact of *Future Shock*, for me, was that for the first time I was a writer in direct communication with an audience.

I had published articles in some of the largest circulation publications in America. Yet the reader response to any magazine article is usually miniscule: a handful of letters, if you are lucky. Even *The Culture Consumers*, which got favorable critical response, and front page treatment in *The New York Times Book Review*, drew no more than a handful of letters. *Future Shock*, on the other hand, opened a torrent of communication from readers. Telephone calls at two in the morning came from readers telling me they had just finished reading the book and would like to discuss various points with me.

■ These are people you didn't know? People who had had no other contact with you at all?

☐ Yes, strangers, total strangers. Absolutely. Excited by what they had read, calling in the middle of the night or morning, frequently long distance, to discuss it, react to it, comment on it, to criticize it, to add personal case histories. People all over the country, and ultimately all over the world, saying things like, "In reading *Future Shock* I felt that you had been looking over my shoulder for the last few years of my life."

Sometimes the reactions were exquisitely personal, like "My husband and I have been discussing relocating the family, but we don't want to destroy our roots. Now I understand why such a move would be disruptive." Sometimes the letters were highly emotional. Like "I was contemplating suicide until I read *Future Shock*..." Or, "You mention the new advances in biology. We have a child suffering from such and such disease. Do you know a scientist who might help us?" Another part of the correspondence was of a more intellectual type. "You didn't give enough weight to population," or genetics, or whatever else—serious discussions of theoretical points. I don't suppose I'm the only writer who gets mail like this, but there was a torrent of it.

■ Then you began lecturing around the country...

□ No, I had been lecturing for many years. When *The Culture Consumers* came out, I was approached by a lecture agent. And from then on I did some lecturing. What happened after *Future Shock* was that the lectures turned into—well, they almost took on the character of political rallies. I was no longer confronted with ordinary audiences, but with standing room crowds, and often there was the sense of—how to put it?—a constituency. It was electric. There were terrific discussions and rap sessions and critiques going on. All of it happening in 1970 and 1971 when the country was alive with continuing reactions to the Sixties, with Vietnam, Nixon in the White House, and all the other dramatic events of the moment.

■ Who were the audiences?

□ Frequently, university audiences. Packed auditoriums at colleges. But not just colleges. Business groups. Professional associations from psychiatrists to bankers.

■ But did anything special distinguish the people who were so animated about *Future Shock*?

□ Yes. They tended, naturally, to be the people who read books. They tended to be young, educated and mostly middle class. But the readership reached far beyond the campus. Young executives. Housewives. Community activists. Teachers. Ministers. Urban planners. Government officials. Parents worried about their long-haired kids.

The success of the book took us by surprise, even the publisher. When the paperback came out, it was the highest priced paperback on the market at that time. But it just rocketed off the racks. The editor-in-chief of Bantam, my paperback publisher, told me that *Future Shock* had an impact on the entire book industry because it was the first time that an intellectual work had achieved such a wide audience in the U.S. It showed it could be done.

Future Shock also touched a nerve and hit the bestseller lists in France, Germany, Japan and more than a dozen other countries. That led to invitations to go to these places and completed my internationalization.

Before that, in 1963, my wife and I had spent a month at the Salzburg Seminar in American Studies. It was the first time we spent any time among European intellectuals. And we came away altered by the experience. I could no longer view things from an exclusively North American perspective.

And, in fact, *Future Shock*, and even more so *The Third Wave*, were written from the standpoint of a trans-national or world audience. The research for the book, the examples chosen, all had that in mind. But the reaction to *Future Shock* completed that process of internationalization, and it also opened many doors, so that we had opportunities to meet with people in many countries— heads of state, Nobel Prize winners, and so forth, all over the world.

■ Where did you meet with heads of state?

□ In Rumania we spent many hours with Ceausescu. In Canada— Trudeau. Whitlam in Australia. Suzuki and Miki in Japan. We were in New Delhi—I had just given a lecture at the National Physical Laboratory—and we got a call from Indira Gandhi, who invited us to come and spend some time with her. And we did. She was quoting *Future Shock* at the time, in her speeches about the need for change.

The surprise to us, I have to say, was that we initially thought that *Future Shock* was a book about people living in high technology societies exposed to extremely rapid rates of technological and social change. We discovered that people living in non-technological societies also felt tremendously pressured by change. Frequently, people living in villages would say, in effect, we feel "future shocked," too.

■ What was your impression of Madame Gandhi?

□ We found it remarkable that, in the midst of all the immediate pressures on her, she would take time out to give us what amounted to an elementary lesson on the geopolitics of the subcontinent. She actually stood in front of a wall-map and lectured us, a bit like a kindly schoolmarm. I suspect there are plenty of people in India who would sneer at that characterization—especially since her recent spasms of authoritarianism. Nevertheless, we had the impression that she actually enjoyed tutoring us—perhaps as a moment of respite from all the heavy tension. Her outer office was filled with army generals.

■ Why?

□ This was exactly the time when East Pakistan broke away from Pakistan and formed Bangladesh. Over six million East Pakistanis by that time had fled the ravages of the Pakistan army and poured over the border into India—something on the order of 10,000,000 refugees by the time it was all over. It was a vast human tragedy, and it was almost hidden from the eyes of the West. Nobody in the U.S. was paying attention at the time, and Nixon, if you recall, was "tilting" toward Pakistan, shipping more arms to the killers.

The Indians were doing their best to feed and house the refugees. In fact, their refugee program, headed by a retired military officer named P.N. Luthra, was extraordinary. I went out and met with him. Luthra himself was in the field 20 hours a day, sleeping in a car. But the conditions were still appalling. And the generals were outside Mrs. Gandhi's office to persuade her that it would be cheaper and easier to go to war against Pakistan than to cope with this tidal wave of fleeing humanity.

■ What was her attitude?

☐ We asked her whether she was going to close off the border. She said that was impossible. That many of the refugees actually had relatives in the Indian population. She couldn't stop the flow. She then surprised us and speculated about her own assassination. She said that if she so much as tried to close off the border, she would be killed. I don't know if she was in a paranoid mood that day, or whether she was referring to some actual plot.

The next day, with her help, I flew off to the border regions east of Calcutta and met with the refugees streaming along the hot dusty roads. I visited their camps and saw them living in concrete sewer pipes stacked three-high as far as the eye could reach. It was harrowing.

So I came back to the United States vowing to get press attention for this incredible tragedy. I had great difficulty getting any of the media to pay attention. I wrote a piece for The New York Times. But I remember going on the Dick Cavett Show at the time and beginning to talk about the tragedy I had just seen. Cavett cut me short, nervously refusing to let me talk about it. After the show he apologized, saying that the subject was a "downer." He said he could mentally hear the viewers' sets clicking off, and he didn't want to lose audience. So he abruptly cut it off. I have never forgotten that—or forgiven it. He had known beforehand that that was what I wanted to talk about on the show.

■ Did you see Mrs. Gandhi again?

☐ Yes, at a soiree in New York attended by a group of American intellectuals—Allen Ginsberg, John Cage, some broadcasters and artists. Brzezinski was there. Max Lerner, Erik Erikson, as I recall. But we found the evening embarrassing, especially after my experience at the refugee camps. The issues raised by some of the people seemed mindlessly trivial—Ginsberg, for example, babbling on about drugs. God knows what she thought of the lot of us! We were depressed by the performance.

■ You seem to use the royal "we" a lot.

□ It's not royal, it's literal I'm a writer and I write alone. I conceptualize my books, and I write them from beginning to end. But I've always had a terrific partner. Heidi is my sounding board for ideas, my severest critic, my editor, and intellectual companion. She often comes with me on lecture tours, often takes questions from the platform, and sometimes lectures on her own. When I travel for research or to attend a meeting or conference, she usually comes not as my wife, but as a full partner or participant. And I've seen her hold her own with heads of state, cabinet ministers, and other big shots from Brazil to Europe.

My by-line is singular because I originate the books and write them. But, for the rest, we usually function together. So the "we" is not royal, it's plural.

■ What themes do the two of you emphasize in these different countries?

□ We usually find ourselves discussing economic development, political implications of rates of change, and everywhere, of course, arguing the case for what I call "anticipatory democracy." We did that in Poland, as well, in 1976, and we were assured by the Party leaders we spoke to that there was no need for any special democratization, anticipatory or otherwise, because once a year Comrade Gierek visits a factory and he, therefore, knows what's on the mind of the workers. So much for Comrade Gierek.*

*Edward Gierek headed the Polish Communist Party from 1970 to 1980, and fell from power with the rise of Solidarity.

In South America, we discussed the future of the Third World. We arrived in Bogotá to discover that passages from *Future Shock* were being broadcast by thirteen jungle radio transmitters to the campesinos—that just took my breath away.

■ Did they explain how this came about?

□ It came about because there was, at that time, a remarkable Monsignor who was running a network of radio transmitters and a printing plant, sending basic public health, sanitation, hygiene, child care, and other survival information to the peasants. And they chose to read passages from *Future Shock* out over those transmitters.

In Japan we were shooting a documentary on *Future Shock* when, in the center of Sapporo, we looked up and saw a file of Western, hippiesque young people marching single file down the street toward us, waving copies of *Future Shock* which they had either bought or been given by their parents. These were Swiss, American, German kids living in the hills around the area where we were filming.

So, we had all kinds of incredible experiences, because the book clearly touched a very personal and political nerve. Needless to say, all this transforms a writer's future. For many people you become something of a guru, which is flattering, but unsettling. I don't like being placed in that role.

THE TELEVISION MEDIUM

■ You've just finished filming again—this time the television program based on *The Third Wave*, right?

□ Yes.

■ Who produced it?

□ Last time, when *Future Shock* was made into a television special, we simply sold the rights to a producer—Metromedia—and we felt we had had very little to say about the resultant product. We had some terrible fights over content with the producer/director, who had his own ideas about what the future might look like and how marvelous technology—all technology—was.

This time Heidi was determined that we should avoid that. So we became directly involved from the start. Since she had a lot to do with organizing the co-production arrangements, and other aspects of the project, she became Executive-in-Charge-of-Production.

The initial impetus, this time, came from NHK, the Japan Broadcasting Corporation, which is the BBC of Japan. They also happen to be the publisher of *The Third Wave* in Japan, and they suggested we make a six- to ten-hour series based on the book.

Fortunately, I had met Galbraith* on a plane just after he had completed making his series. I asked how long it had taken and what his reaction was. He said three years, and his summary statement was typical Galbraith. "One word," he confided, "is worth a thousand pictures."

■ Is that your reaction too?

☐ No. But we weren't willing to spend three years working on a series based on a book that I had already finished. So we limited it to one program. It ended up with NHK co-producing with us together with TVOntario, the leading educational network in Canada.

It was a true multicultural production, from the ground up. We had Japanese, Canadians and Americans involved in every step. When crews went to shoot, all three were represented, usually with local people as well from the country we were in. We shot in nine countries.

■ What was your role?

☐ I was the host narrator, and, with a lot of collective tutoring, I wrote the script.

*Economist John Kenneth Galbraith, whose television series was shown in many countries.

■ How does it differ from the book?

☐ Television can do many things a book cannot—and vice versa. As a writer, I found the collaborative enterprise—the business of being dependent on others to translate one's idea and images—constraining. Even though the people I worked with were terrific—no tantrums, no temperament, just hard work, long hours and a devoted attempt to convey the ideas in the book. Even so, the demands of the medium are enormous and the technical constraints formidable.

We used the most advanced computer graphics. We had the best camera and very sophisticated audio equipment. The edit rooms looked like Houston Mission Control.

The results are, I think, elegant. There is visual poetry along with a great many ideas. But television is not a medium that comes easily or naturally for most authors.

■ Because you are print oriented?

☐ No doubt. But Heidi and I are inveterate, absolute cinema nuts. We go to the movies every chance we get. In every country, in every language. So the chance to use television to convey complex ideas in a non-pandering, serious, yet visually stunning way—that was the challenge.

■ But what does the program say? Were you able to convey your political and social ideas despite the constraints of the television form?

☐ Certainly. The program is political, in the broadest sense. It argues, as my books do, that our entire political apparatus is obsolete, that we may even have to question our constitutions, even our assumptions about majority rule, and that we will need to reconceptualize human rights. It also discusses the need for fundamental change in our education system, and the need for social supports for the millions of people in dying traditional industries.

It has startling effects, and it moves at a breakneck pace, but it also deals with serious issues, from centralization and energy, to family life, privacy, pollution, economic development in the poor countries, and the economic crisis in the high technology nations.

■ Has making this program altered your views about television?

☐ Of course, there's only so much you can say in a visual mode. It has power. But it also has powerful limitations. You have so little time to develop ideas logically...

Even written narration. Listen closely the next time you watch an American documentary news show. Chances are the narration is telegraphic—clipped.

Words like "and" and "or," words like "therefore"—in short, words that, in written language, establish logical relationships—are often omitted in television language. As a result, many logical relationships are left undefined.

One reason for this is technical. Narration comes in short bursts, while the visuals flow by. Dropping the logic terms makes it easier for the editor to position the narration vis-à-vis the pictures. Pictures win. Logic loses. Visuals also determine the pace of the narration, so many qualifications and reservations tend to get squeezed.

■ But television has its own power—not just the fact that it can reach millions of people.

☐ Absolutely. We have a beautiful sequence, for example, of a space shot dissolving into a flower, or of a lovely little girl running through the fields—these have the symbolic power of poetry. They convey many ideas simultaneously through connotation. I love the play of visual associations.

■ Any other lessons?

☐ Many. Among them the degree to which deception is possible. It is possible to fake backgrounds, sync sounds, use editing to divert attention from deleted material, and to play a thousand other games. Of course, we all know how newspapers can slant stories or position them, and otherwise incorporate editorial bias in what seems like straight reportage. I think, however, that this is more common in television—not so much in the interests of some political point of view, as in the effort to "entertain" the viewership.

Moreover, a whole new generation of video technology is beginning to appear which will make it even easier for the director and/or editor to create images almost from whole cloth. I went to see the Disney film, TRON, which is intellectually boring but an electronic *tour de force.* It begins to hint at the kind of things that can be done with computer animation and imaging.

In making *The Third Wave* we actually used a piece of advanced computer animation equipment before it was released to the marketplace. Many of our effects were done on the engineering prototype of this equipment. It lets you take any image—a drawing, a photo, or even an object like a beer can—and convert that into an almost infinite number of other images, so that a cow can be transformed into an abstract painting and the abstract painting into a moving, gyrating image.

Eventually, I have to assume that less and less actual shooting is going to be done on location. Many images will be created electronically in the studio. We'll take a shot of a real person—it might even be the President—and be able, electronically, to set that still photo into motion. You'll be able to create a tape of the President of the United States doing anything you like—throwing a cream pie at a political opponent, or, for that matter, accepting a bribe. The studio technicians already call it "scene simulation." What are the implications of that?

■ What does it do to our sense of reality?

☐ What does it do to reality itself? After all, the simulation of reality is a part of reality. It's like an infinite progression of mirrors.

The rapid development of these video techniques, especially in combination with computers, new forms of image and data storage, is likely to have an impact not simply on entertainment, or on documentaries, or on information in the general sense, but on the way we think—the levels we think on—and our very perception of ourselves in the universe.

And what does that do to the future?

9 A FAR CRY FROM DELPHI

One of the most widely misunderstood intellectual developments in recent decades has been the rise of "futurism."

In countries from China to Venezuela there now are think-tanks devotedly studying tomorrow. The U.S.-based World Future Society claims tens of thousands of members, ranging from corporate planners and radical ecologists to teachers and computer experts.

Critics deride the enterprise, often singling out some great event, like the oil embargo, and then, with a show of merriment, pointing out that this or that futurist failed to "predict" it.

Serious futurists, in turn, are amused at the criticism, for most of them do not regard themselves as being in the "prediction business." They spend much of their time studying the present, suggesting policy options to decision-makers, pointing out the otherwise unnoticed risks, options and consequences of decisions— and uttering precious few "prophecies." Likewise human beings in any field, they know what they do not—and cannot—know.

A far cry, indeed, from the Oracle at Delphi!

—A.T.

■ Because *Future Shock* and *The Third Wave* both, in part, deal with the future, you are often referred to as a "futurist." Does the term aptly describe you? Is it how you see yourself? And does it mean the same thing to you as to the people who label you a "futurist"?

□ I do not reject the term "futurist." I think it's a perfectly respectable designation, but I do not regard myself as primarily a "futurist." I regard myself as primarily a writer, an author, and a social critic.

I don't believe in art for art's sake, and I don't believe in history for history's sake. Nor do I believe in the future for future's sake—in the sense of some disembodied curiosity about tomorrow's world. "Looking into the future," which no one can do, except in a metaphorical sense, is a way of improving decisions in the present.

Of course, I don't believe anybody can "know" the future. People who pretend they can, as far as I am concerned, are in the category of newspaper astrologers and quacks. However, I don't believe that any of us could survive for even ten minutes, unless we devoted a significant part of our mental activity to making assumptions about the future.

When I reach for a cup of coffee, I am making an implicit assumption about the future—that the cup will still be there on the table when my fingers reach it. That is a very short range forecast, of course, but it is nevertheless an assumption about a state of affairs in the future. And just as individuals continually make such assumptions, whole cultures share certain powerful images of the future.

Every culture has, in my judgment, a different bias toward time. Some are heavily biased toward the past. In them, children are brought up to think that wisdom and knowledge lie in the past—and for some cultures that is, in fact, largely correct. In a culture which changes at an extremely slow pace, enduring for hundreds, even thousands of years in the same ecological niche, with the same social arrangements and the same technologies, it is probably true that the smartest thing a child can do is to imitate what his or her father or mother did, and, in turn, what *their* parents did. Parental wisdom will usually be more perfect than that of the present generation because the know-how of the older generation has been honed by thousands of years of practice.

However, in a changing society and culture, particularly in a period of revolutionary change such as we find ourselves in today, the past becomes a less sure guide to present decisions and future possibilities. In this circumstance, thinking clearly about future possibilities and creating new ideas to cope with them becomes essential to survival. The time-bias of the culture must shift toward increased future-consciousness.

In general, everyone's head is filled with assumptions about the future as well as about the past. How we manipulate those two sets of assumptions heavily determines our conscious decisions in the present. This manipulation must change as circumstances change. To a degree, that is what my book, *Future Shock,* is about.

■ But surely how we act in the present also affects the future. Even our projections influence it. We make self-fulfilling and self-negating prophecies.

☐   Yes. For me the best examples are still Huxley and Orwell, who projected an industrial future so bleak and regimented that they helped contribute to the pressures against it. Their image of the future was essentially a linear projection of classical industrial society—Second Wave civilization. They did not foresee the dialectical swing that the Third Wave implies. Nevertheless, they were men of great genius and their warnings served us extremely well.

■ But can't the same argument be applied to you as well—that is, that your own projections of the future may influence it to some degree?

☐ I hope so. At least in some small degree.

THE FOUNDERS OF FUTURISM

■ Is the future you project in *The Third Wave* essentially fixed and immutable? Should we make plans based upon the inevitability of that future, or are you saying there are a whole host of possible projections and that the future you describe in *The Third Wave* is only one, the one you regard as most likely or perhaps most preferable?

□ Let's not confuse the preferable with the probable. Certainly, I am a social critic, not a neutral prognosticator. I don't write to read my own words, but to communicate with large numbers of people. The purpose of that is to encourage fresh, novel ways of looking at reality and also to smooth the way for social changes that I, as the author, regard as desirable.

However, there is no single future waiting for us out there—only multiple possibilities. In fact, this idea of plural futures is absolutely central to most futurist thinking today.

Before we get to that, though, it may be interesting to look at the recent social history of the future. The word "futurist" has a checkered past. Perhaps the first modern use occurred in the arts. At the beginning of the twentieth century a school of painters, poets, and sculptors arose in Western Europe, mainly in Italy, who called themselves "futurists." They issued a manifesto, wrote lengthy essays, and created an aesthetic ideology around the term.

Poets like Marinetti, painters like Severini, sculptors like Boccioni glorified the machine and all it stood for. But in Italy and elsewhere, these artists, who began by being fascinated with speed, action, and technology, also began to glorify violence, war, and ultimately fascism.

As these ideas became discredited, the term "futurist" largely disappeared from intellectual discourse—and then popped up again in an entirely new form after World War II. It began with a man named Ossip Flechtheim, in Germany, who started writing about the need to forecast the future and the need to teach what he called "futurology" in the schools. (That term, which sounds awful in English, and somehow connotes quackery, has quite different, less negative, associations in German and other languages.)

By the 1960s, a group of other scholars, writers, and journalists, including myself, began calling for more systematic attention to the long-range implications of change. They, or we, came from widely different backgrounds, and carried many different ideological labels. The journalist Robert Jungk in Germany and Austria—a small "d" democrat and anti-fascist—travelled the world urging the humanization of the future. Gaston Berger in France began a journal called *Prospective*. A lonely historian in the Soviet Union began writing about the future under the pseudonym Bestuzhev-Lada. A Dutch Senator named Fred Polak wrote a massive historical survey of cultural attitudes toward the future. A Scot named John McHale and his Hungarian-born wife and colleague, Magda Cordell, began working with Buckminster Fuller on a detailed study of future resource needs. Kenneth Boulding, the economist and systems thinker, Olaf Helmer, the mathematician and philosopher at the Rand Corp., Ted Gordon, the space engineer, Herman Kahn, the physicist, Jim Dator, the political scientist, Daniel Bell, the sociologist, were all drawn toward the study of the future. My own systematic interest began at about the same time—and by 1965 I had begun writing about it. By 1966, I was teaching a course at the New School for Social Research called the "sociology of the future."

The man whose work influenced most of us, was Bertrand de Jouvenel—the stepson of Colette, who once worked as a rum-runner in Louisiana, later worked as a journalist, and subsequently wrote profound and scholarly works on political science, economics, and on the whole notion of forecasting. He created an organization called Futuribles, still operating in France under the direction of his son, Hugues. Today, anyone who has worked seriously in this field is familiar with his *The Art of Conjecture*. De Jouvenel is really the one who introduced the word "futures" into the language. That is, for de Jouvenel and most futurists today there isn't a future. There are futures—plural. There is, at any given instant, an array of possible futures. Within that array of possible futures, there is a smaller set of plausible or probable futures. And finally, within that set, there is a still smaller sub-set of preferable futures.

Some writers about the future emphasize the possible. Science fiction writers, for example, spell out a very wide range of *possible futures.* In contrast, forecasters who work for governments or for corporations are typically concerned with *probable futures*. They tend to regard most writing about possible futures as utopian or dystopian but not very practical. They try to determine the odds that some particular state of affairs will actually come to pass. They focus narrowly on those futures that seem to them most likely. But even they are usually careful to hedge their bets. They would be the first to admit the impossibility of accurately "predicting" the future in the usual sense of that word.

STRAIGHT-LINE THINKERS

■ What about their methods?

□ Some of them are no more than straight-line extrapolators. In whatever field—technology, economics, energy, resources, population—they try to identify trends that exist in today's world, and then simply extrapolate them, insisting, in effect, that whatever processes are at work today, whatever institutions exist today, will continue to exist or operate tomorrow, only more so, or less so.

I suspect most corporations that claim to be engaged in planning are, in fact, engaged in nothing more than this kind of linear extrapolation, an extremely weak and unimaginative method.

On the surface, extending today's trends seems safe and scientific. Yet it is often neither. Straight-line extrapolation works far better in periods of stability than in periods of revolutionary upheaval, like the present.

I don't much believe all those extrapolators who tell us that world per capita income has been rising by "x" for 10 years, therefore it will be "y" by the year 2000. Or that population will hit 7 billion because it has been rising at a certain rate. Unless there is some model to explain why something is going to happen, the forward projection of existing trends is very risky.

This form of "forecasting" usually looks neutral or free of bias. Yet straight-line projection is just as subject to bias as any other form of forecasting or speculation.

First, there is the question of what to extrapolate? What trends are worth monitoring? That choice is value-laden. Then there are cultural or ideological biases. When you look at corporate or government planning, for example, you find that most of it is heavily econo-centric, as though the economy were the only thing worth monitoring.

In fact, there is a further, hidden bias based on the kinds of data that are available and deemed valid. Government and corporate think tanks of the so-called right, left, or center, extrapolate from pre-existent statistics which themselves are biased. Our existing statistical data-base, as people like Bertram Gross pointed out in the sixties, overemphasizes economic data and underemphasizes or even ignores critical social, cultural, psychological, or political variables that are typically harder to measure. The net result is that while they try to give their forecasts, their appraisals of probable futures, a quantitative "look," the numbers very often mask spongy data and ill thought through assumptions.

■ Can you give us examples of some other futurist methods?

☐ There are many non-extrapolative methods in use as well. There are attempts to class possible future events in terms of the degree to which they are mutually reinforcing or mutually inhibiting. There are contingency plans—the U.S. military maintains between 50 and 60 large-scale contingency plans for events that may never happen. There are attempts to classify possible events in terms of impact, so that some are rated as "low probability, but high impact" and others as the reverse. There are methods that involve small groups of experts, and others that depend on the participation of large numbers of non-experts.

There are sectoral efforts aimed at studying the future of technology, for example, or the potential social impact of new communication systems. There is an effort underway in the Hawaii judiciary to identify public issues that may affect the courts and the legal system a decade or more from now. There are "anticipatory democracy" groups in many communities—more all the time—that attempt to involve citizens in state-wide or community-wide goal setting. Clem Bezold of the Institute for Alternative Futures in Washington, D.C., monitors these efforts, and also works systematically to introduce longer range concerns into the legislative process in Congress and the state legislatures. The Congressional Clearinghouse on the Future is composed of members of Congress sympathetic to this legislative futurism.

The methods, organizational designs, goals and procedures of these efforts vary widely. Almost none are designed to produce what are commonly called "predictions." Yet all of them try to piece together an imaginative picture of future states of the world or some part of it. They may start by postulating an event in the future, and then work back from that event—if that event were to occur, what would have had to have happened first to have made it possible? By asking that question again and again, they, in effect, arrive at a scenario of change.

■ Where do you fit in all this? How do you go about your own work?

☐ Myself, I come from a different background. I do not come out of either mathematics or physics, or "social physics" for that matter. While I see considerable value in systematic and quantified analysis of social and economic change, and I respect the work of many who use these methods, I also recognize the enormous limitations of this style of work.

Put differently, I think we should make maximum use of all the quantitative tools—all the statistics and systematic models and computer aids. But once we have, I think we should remain skeptical of the results.

Such methods can be a source of great insight. They can reveal or illuminate previously unnoticed relationships. They can reveal trends. They can simulate a wide range of possibilities.

But they do not deliver "truth," and precisely because they come wrapped in numbers, they can be doubly misleading. In the end, all futurism, like all historiography (including what is called cliometrics), is inevitably impregnated with at least a touch of subjectivity.

Futurism is an art, not a form of engineering. So I can sum up my view simply:

Use science in support of art.

Remember, too, that I come from a tradition which places great respect on first-hand observation and reporting. For many years I was a reporter, a journalist.

Reading books, technical and scholarly papers and journals is essential to me, and I do a lot of it. But unlike many specialists, who have been taught to ignore their own raw experience in favor of the printed page, I also use real-life encounters, personal impressions, travel and face-to-face interviews with relevant people to help me set the statistics and academic studies into perspective. I am not a scientist or a pseudo-scientist. And I labor under no illusion that what I write is somehow antiseptic—political, morally, or socially neutral.

10 ON INTELLECTUAL TOOLS

We are all bombarded by stimuli from outside our skin. *Physical stimuli affect taste, touch and smell; cognitive stimuli strike us in the form of ideas, information, images, symbols. News blares at us from the car radio. Snippets of television, magazine ads, telephone messages, headlines—all are somehow blocked out or stored away in memory.*

The way we organize this endless, incoming flow of data is crucial, however, not merely for daily life, but even more so for management decision-making, for education, for political organizing and a thousand other activities.

To shape the emergent future, we will need powerful new intellectual tools—new theories of change and causation capable of explaining the new social and political complexity; new categories and classification systems; and new models to help us interrelate the disparate, discordant data that now threatens to drown us in meaninglessness.

Like many machines of the smokestack era, our intellectual tools, too, are ready for the museum.

In this conversation, we briefly examine some of the tools I find useful—my methods of work and some of the premises behind them.

—A.T.

■ As an author you assemble a mass of data. On what basis do you reject some data as irrelevant, while emphasizing other data as critical? How do you develop a clear picture from a muddle of facts?

□ The true answer—not just for me, but for everybody—must include the word "hunch" or the more elegant term "intuition." Hunch or intuition is an inescapable element in this work, no matter how hard the number crunchers may try to disguise it. We all rely on our viscera. But not just on viscera. All of us, and here I mean all human beings, not just writers or futurists—all of us also create models of reality. When confronted with a mass of data, the human mind creates a model—in fact, multiple models—which help us to order and manipulate, that is, make sense of the data. Most writers do not make their models explicit and may even be unaware of the models they are applying. But there is no escape from the need for modeling reality.

I think you can actually identify implicit models in the work of many authors—Balzac and Zola, for example, come to mind—not to mention the work of social thinkers, whether Adam Smith, Freud, or Marx. Of course, writers' models not only tend to be implicit, they need not be as rigorous and precise as those used in science, and the imperatives of the model are sometimes bent or adjusted to take account of the imperatives of dramatic presentation. But there are models—often highly complex models—nonetheless.

■ How do you arrive at your models?

□ No one can answer that sort of question completely because there is often an unconscious element in model building, not to mention an unavoidable mass of unsurfaced assumptions. Setting that aside, I usually begin with my research notes and materials. These, bear in mind, are often quite massive. They may represent five or more years of voracious reading—technical journals, foreign newspapers, academic papers, letters, statistical summaries, reports from many countries, as well as insights picked up from novels, films or poetry, along with typed, usually verbatim interviews with experts in fields as disparate as economics and military strategy, robotics, music, or child-care.

I start by shuffling and rearranging all this material into various categories, searching for interrelations and other patterns in it. I normally allow the model to emerge from this process. It derives from the material. Once a model emerges, then, as additional research material comes in, it either fits into the model, or the model has to be adjusted, expanded, limited, or jettisoned. Sometimes I work the other way. I start with a tentative model and then do the research and alter the model as the data dictates.

■ How did you work in the case of *The Third Wave*?

□ In the case of *The Third Wave* I began with a partial model of social change and of social structure. The writing of the book was also a process of continually elaborating and completing the model. But once you develop and apply a useful model, it begins to organize the material for you so that certain relationships and implications which were otherwise hidden become clear. From that you derive tentative conclusions. Clearly it's a very complicated internal, intellectual process by which any writer arrives at the written word.

As for my own work on social change, I start with the assumption that social events and phenomena are interrelated and not isolated, so that change doesn't come packaged as it does in the academic disciplines. You can't have an economic change without changes in family life, energy, and ecological systems. All these things are hooked together and connected by complex feedback loops. So I focus strongly on the search for interrelationships.

I also start with the assumption that there is no single driving force in history, that it is governed, rather, by the *convergence* of forces or tendencies that produce major changes.

FLUCTUATIONS AND REVOLUTIONS

■ Give me an example.

□ All right. I'll choose one at random: the Stalin trials in the 1930s. I am just now reading a remarkable piece of social and political history, *On A Field Of Red,* by Anthony Cave Brown and Charles

McDonald. In this book they describe the rise of Hitler and Stalin, the German inflation, the coming of Roosevelt—really the entire history of the period. And at one point they explain the series of treason trials in which Stalin wiped out almost all his top generals and military officers. Cave Brown and McDonald point out that this reduction in Soviet military capacity came precisely at the moment that Hitler was rapidly expanding German military capacity, and so, at that moment, what my friend, Ilya Prigogine* would call an internal fluctuation (the trials) coincided with an external fluctuation (Hitler's rise). When I see connections between internal changes and changes occurring outside, I ask whether one might not reinforce the other.

What Prigogine says, as I understand it, is that any phenomenon, whether it is a chemical compound or a social system, is always undergoing internal change, always fluctuating, so to speak. Each phenomenon or system has its own internal sub-systems which are continually vibrating or fluctuating. Occasionally, one of these fluctuations reaches an amplitude sufficient to shatter the overall structure. Often, however, it is necessary that several fluctuations in different sub-systems converge and reinforce one another before the larger structure is substantially altered or revolutionized.

In addition, every phenomenon has an external environment. Fluctuations occur in the external environment as well, and a large external fluctuation may coincide with the conjuncture of several internal fluctuations to make the system even more vulnerable to transformation or revolutionary changes.

*Prigogine, born in Moscow in 1917, won the Nobel Prize in 1977 for his work in physical chemistry. He heads the International Institutes for Physics and Chemistry in Brussels and the Center for Statistical Mechanics and Thermodynamics at the University of Texas at Austin. His work on the thermodynamics of non-equilibrium systems has implications that reach far beyond physics or chemistry.

Under certain circumstances, Prigogine says, the crack-up of one structure, as a consequence of one or more fluctuations, leads to the formation of a new, more complex structure which requires more energy to sustain it. He calls this a "dissipative structure."

In human terms, I believe something analogous is happening. We are moving to new, more differentiated social structures that need more information to sustain them. So this part of Prigogine's theory of fluctuations greatly interests me.

Many social and economic conditions lend themselves to this kind of formulation. For example, all the industrialized nations today are undergoing powerful internal transformations partly caused by the technological revolution. This *internal* upheaval, which is reflected in the decline of industries like auto and steel and the rise of wholly new industries like computers and genetics, is reinforced and accelerated by *external* pressures generated by the rising militancy of the non-industrial countries, the temporary cohesion of OPEC, etc. It is the convergence of many internal and external forces that builds up the pressure for a revolutionary restructuring of the high tech economies. The result is the emergence of Third Wave economies at a higher, far more complex level of development, but far more dependent on information.

THE UNI-DIMENSIONAL MARX

■ Can't an analogy be drawn between your approach to social change and Marx's model?

□ The differences are more pronounced than the similarities. I was a Marxist in my twenties. But the more I came to know of society, the more I observed first-hand as a journalist, and the more rapidly change transformed the high technology societies, the more outmoded and misleading I found Marxist theory to be.

When I was young, the Marxist explanation of how society works came as a thrilling revelation. Marx was a towering genius. He reminded me of Bach, in the fugal complexity of his thought.

And, whether aware of it or not, even those who despise Marx have, in fact, been influenced by him, just as we have been influenced by Newton, Darwin, and Freud and the other great intellects who shaped our perception of the world.

After Marx, it was no longer possible to think of technology in the same way as before. It was no longer possible to ignore class. It was no longer possible to see history as an unbroken continuity. It was no longer possible to see politics and economics as separate, airtight categories. To be ignorant of Marx in today's world is to be semi-literate. Half the population of the planet treats his words as scripture. But Marx, himself, was an expression of classical Second Wave or industrial society, formed by its assumptions—and many of these assumptions simply no longer hold true.

My work today still focusses strongly on issues he wrote about: social change, the role of technology, conflict, discontinuity, and revolution in the broadest sense. But there are crucial differences between my present position and that of Marxism.

One key difference has to do with the primacy Marxism assigns to the economy.

■ A Marxist might agree that the economy is a system and that it has an internal motion. But the Marxist would insist that all the other systems in society are subordinate to the economy. You seem to be making a major break with Marxism over this issue, by making the economy only one among many sub-systems. Was this difference the root of your break with Marxism?

□ Yes, for the Marxists the non-economic is only a "super-structure" built on a techno-economic base. And I do differ with this. But this was not the main cause of my break with Marxism.

My intellectual break with Marxism came ages ago when the forecasts made by American Marxists were so brutally contradicted by everyday reality. At the end of World War II, when I was a student, Marxists insisted that the United States was on the brink of a great economic depression, a recurrence of the 1930s. They said it was only a matter of time before "the general crisis of capitalism" overtook the United States. What followed was, in fact, the affluent 50s and 60s. And there were other false forecasts derived from the Marxist model. The American working class was not "immiserated." Social cleavages along lines of sex, age, and race seemed to me far more important in the U.S. than those of class, and the attempt to explain them all in terms of class analysis subordinated reality to theory.

If all the powerful machinery of theoretical Marxism could be trained on the United States and come up with answers that were so dead wrong, one had to question its more general validity as a tool for either understanding or creating change. On top of this, evidence from many countries, not just the "special case" of the USSR, proved inescapably that the "dictatorship of the proletariat" is exactly that: a dictatorship.

Intellectually, it became clearer to me that Marxism was a misleading, obsolete tool for understanding reality in the high-technology world. Using Marxism to diagnose the inner structure of high technology societies today is like limiting oneself to a magnifying glass in the age of the electron microscope.

■ Are you saying that class conflict is not central to change today? Or are you saying it is no longer the key issue in high technology countries, though it may still be the dominant issue in other societies?

□ Dominant, no, not at all. Technology and the economy are important, but they aren't the "base" upon which everything else is mere "superstructure." After all the verbiage is hauled away—and Marx, of course, is a lot cleverer than his followers, so he covers his tracks better—after all is said and done, Marx insists that the basic source of change in society is either the class struggle or, more generally, the advance of technology and concomitant changes in economic relationships. The advance of the "means of production" leads to changes in the "social relations of production," etc.

There may well be societies in which a class analysis is still useful for elementary understanding, to be sure—where there is one class desperately oppressing another and these economic fault lines are very sharp, so that class conflict is the dominant conflict within the society *at that particular moment*. But to generalize that, to universalize it, to insist on its primacy, and to claim it applies at all times, *a priori*, in all class societies, is to me a terrible and tragic mistake.

There are societies today in which class conflict is raw and decisive—and in which many other conflicts are subordinate. But, for me, that is a temporary, not permanent condition. And even when that is true, there are big variations with respect to how dominant, or how salient, the class conflict is compared with racial, ethnic, intergenerational, and other conflicts. Marx reduced all these other conflicts to relative insignificance in all societies after "primitive communalism" and before "communism." His emphasis on class was Eurocentric and extrapolated from his own period of early capitalism. The monomania about class helps account for the failures of Marxist theory in country after country.

■ I would agree that to assume *a priori* that class analysis will reveal all one needs to know about a society, or that class conflict is the only central conflict in a society is a serious error. But it also seems wrong to deny that class analysis is one powerful tool for understanding modern society, and class struggle one critical form of conflict. I assume you don't imply such a denial.

□ No, my point is that while Marx's original analysis was intellectually stunning, for all its breathtaking complexity, it was and is uni-dimensional.

■ Uni-dimensional? Whether you agree with its findings or not, Marxism is a broad, all-encompassing theory that has things to say about every aspect of life.

□ True, but class conflict is only one of the basic tensions in society, and to wrap an entire theory of history around it is to examine a complex phenomenon through a single slit.

One could write the entire history of human society in terms of sexual conflict—one thinks immediately of Freud or some modern feminists—or in terms of racial conflict, community conflict, political conflict, etc. One might wish to divide society into various sectors, along multiple axes of conflict, and show how these interrelate. Under certain circumstances, that would yield, in my judgment, a less econo-centric, more multi-dimensional tool for understanding—and even for changing—society.

The point is that there are other, equally revealing models, depending upon what one is trying to arrive at, and there is no single sure-fire omni-explanatory model.

■ Including your own Third Wave model?

□ Obviously.

THE THIRD WAVE MODEL

■ How would you describe the Third Wave model? If not from class or other conflicts, then where does it start?

□ I begin in a more or less inductive or empirical fashion by identifying what all civilizations seem to have in common. For example, all civilizations have some kind of energy system. They all have some method for producing the goods and services necessary for survival. They all have some system for distributing those goods and services. The energy system, the production system and the distribution system are all obviously very closely tied together, and together they can be said to form a "techno-sphere."

All civilizations also have an ecology, as it were, of social institutions—a "socio-sphere." Within different civilizations, these organizations or institutions are related to each other in diverse ways. In ours, for example, we find that the nuclear family prepares the child for life in a mass education school, which prepares the young person for life in the corporation or the socialist production enterprise. So within what I call the socio-sphere, there are different interacting sub-systems.

The techno-sphere and the socio-sphere are tightly interconnected.

All civilizations also have systems for the communication of information. Some societies don't require much information exchange and so they send runners across the countryside or they create, as the Persians did, towers on which a man with big lungs would shout to the man in the next tower, and, in this way, pass along the message. But little communication was necessary outside the local village, and so systems of communication were underdeveloped. Nevertheless, all societies have some sort of communication structure, rudimentary or not, and I call that the "info-sphere."

Again, the info-sphere is tightly wired into the techno- and socio-spheres.

Moreover, all societies operate within a "bio-sphere," and conditions within this bio-sphere may vary dramatically from time to time for any civilization. All civilizations also have a "power-sphere," in which authority is allocated through both formal and informal political institutions. And, ultimately, all societies also have what might be called a "psycho-sphere"—a sphere of intimate relationships, of subjectivity, of personality.

Put all these together—techno-sphere, socio-sphere, info-sphere, bio-sphere, power-sphere, and psycho-sphere—and they encompass much (not all) of what goes on in any civilization or society. With this breakdown, you can begin systematically canvassing the interactions, both within and between these various spheres of action.

■ Where do you locate culture—in the info-sphere?

□ No. Culture, in a sense, is another slice, as we'll see in a moment. For now I just want to stress that, within each sphere there are complicated internal parts, all closely interrelated, all continually changing, fluctuating, developing. Each of these spheres can be analyzed, its components and their linkages described in greater detail, if we choose to do so.

At the same time, it is also clear that the spheres themselves are continually changing, and that they are interrelated in a system of mutual dependence. Their relationships, only hinted at in *The Third Wave*, could also be sketched in greater detail.

One could, if we wanted to, spell out not only the "meta-relationships" among the different spheres and the "micro-relationships" within each sphere, but the "tele-relationships" that exist between elements of one sphere and elements of another. In short, the model can be made as complex and detailed as we wish, and can be organized at any level of abstraction. It can store and interrelate a vast amount of information, ordering it for us so we can use it.

This model helps us examine any civilization and differentiate among civilizations. But it is also highly fluid. It permits us to see the various elements of a society as they come into being, usually as part of a wave of associated, inter-stimulating changes. This is why I use the wave metaphor.

Instead of presenting history as a sequence of "stages," as though each were a still photograph, the social wave theory allows us to view whole societies in process. For example, we can see more than a single wave of change passing through the same society at the same time. In Japan the family system is still moving toward nuclear form. It's part of the Second Wave of change—the wave of traditional industrialization completing itself, so to speak. But simultaneously, we see many aspects of the Third Wave starting up.

So instead of seeing a society as unitary, we picture it as made of concurrent movements, waves of associated changes. Societies can be compared in terms of the mix of First, Second, or Third Wave elements, and in terms of the different rates of change in each. And so forth. The wave model is based on process, not structure alone.

But it goes without saying that civilizations are highly complex processes, and what I've described so far is still only part of the actual model I used in writing *The Third Wave*.

■ In your work, you speak of structural changes. But you also refer to "civilizational principles." How do these fit into your Third Wave model?

☐ Yes. The various spheres I've described are what might be called the structural elements in any civilization. They are plugged together in various complex ways. But there is another dimension entirely that, so to speak, cuts across all these spheres. For example, every civilization also develops its own "super-ideology" to justify itself, to explain its place in history and the universe, and to vindicate or rationalize its operations. And that is the cultural overlay that covers the whole and helps shape its structure. That ideology is reflected in all the spheres, from family life to technology.

In addition, every civilization seems to operate according to certain identifiable principles which are part of its culture. In industrial civilization, which is the one to which I most systematically apply this model, all of these spheres are affected by the principles of standardization, synchronization, specialization, centralization, concentration, maximization, etc., the basic organizing principles of industrialized societies.

■ Where the "leftist" approach uses sexual, racial, and economic or social relations and like concepts as organizing principles, the "wave" approach focusses on principles like standardization or synchronization. Isn't this very abstract?

☐ Perhaps, but it is also very concrete and, I think, far more comprehensive. When we put all these pieces together, not as fixed elements in a civilizational jig-saw puzzle, but as changing, cinematic elements, we get something approximating a whole, all the parts of which are developing, interacting, reinforcing one another, moving synchronously with one another—or, alternatively, counterbalancing, offsetting, or colliding with one another. Conflicts over racism, sexism, or class, however important, are simply not enough to describe a whole society or civilization and where it is going.

A civilization is made up of people living their lives, going about their daily routines, fighting, loving, dying, giving birth. The child brushing his teeth in the morning (before going off to school to be prepared for a lifetime of factory or office work) is as much a representative of our civilization as the great artists or political leaders who fill the museums and the history books.

If we look closely at the way the child is reared; at the degree of standardization in his or her life; at the synchronization of his/her departure for school in the morning with the rest of the family's schedule; at the mass movement of other pupils; if we examine the technology and energy on which his daily life is dependent; the institution of the school and its relationship to the state, the family, the church; if we examine the communications media that shape the child, the physical environment he/she lives in; the political power structure into which he/she is born—we see the whole civilization crystallized, as it were, in a single concrete individual.

In this way, the model I have developed, with its various "spheres" and "principles" and its "super-ideology," is linked to actual life. It is not just some abstract, academic, antiseptic model, but one that is directly related to behavior. It helps explain what makes us tick.

And, for me, this model has certain powerful advantages.

■ Certainly we need models to understand society. You divide up the system into the various spheres you emphasize because any society must have them, in however rudimentary a form. But one might also divide up society in quite a different way. For example, any society must have a political decision-making system, an economic system for production and consumption; a kinship sphere for defining gender roles, sexual, and socialization relations; and what might be called a community system or sphere for defining religious, ethnic, and racial identities.

Cutting the system up in terms of these categories would focus attention on social relationships and on social groups that have identities as historical agents of change—and, after all, it is, for the most part, people organized into movements who make history.

So why choose the spheres you focus on, rather than these others which are rooted more directly in the basic needs of daily life, and around which social movements organize for change—politics, economics, race or culture, and sex?

☐ I certainly wouldn't argue against alternative models. No model is complete. The question is which model serves best for a particular purpose. The Third Wave model is designed to be as embracing as possible, and to be clarifying, to help us structure as much otherwise seemingly unrelated data as possible.

I don't begin with the rather Marxist idea that history is made by social movements. For example, the scientists on the Manhattan Project clearly "made history" when they invented the first nuclear bomb. Yet they hardly qualify as a "social movement" in your sense. So building a model around specific social movements or the axes around which they form may be revealing for some purposes, but it seems too constraining to me.

In addition, while I don't want to beat this question of models to death, there is one other aspect of the Third Wave model that is worth mentioning. And that is that it is built around conflict and it does have implications for conflict theory.

A THEORY OF CONFLICT

■ Some futurists picture the arrival of "post-industrial society" as a more or less smooth process. You don't.

☐ Right. I don't picture the emerging world as conflict-free, nor the process of reaching it. On the contrary, I see us entering a period of fierce social and political conflict. To understand that—whether on a global scale or within our society—we need a theory of conflict.

■ What would such a theory of conflict do?

☐ It would help us see the relationships among different, seemingly isolated or independent conflicts. And it would help us prioritize them, so we focus attention on the main ones.

■ You have spoken about the wave model as providing that kind of insight. You speak, for example, about the "super-struggle." Can you explain the theory of conflict that flows out of your waves-of-change model?

☐ First, when I speak of a "wave" of historic change sweeping across a society, I am not speaking of a single specific change—in technology, for example. I am speaking of a whole chain of associated changes that reinforce one another and accelerate one another and move the system in a definable direction.

That began to happen with the First Wave of change—the spread of agriculture. A new way of life spread with its own new social, political and religious institutions, its own principles for coping with the environment around it.

When the industrial revolution launched the Second Wave of change, it, too, began spreading a new way of life and new institutions, values and principles which came into intense conflict with the existing First Wave institutions of agricultural civilization.

Naturally, the notion of waves is merely a metaphor. Making those waves of change are people, individuals, organized groups, armies, churches, research laboratories, businessmen, political parties, and so on.

Those whose economic and other interests arose from the agricultural way of life found themselves fighting off the "upstart" groups who were creating the industrial revolution.

So much is fairly familiar. What's more interesting is the idea that a single society can have several waves of change running through it simultaneously, coming into conflict, and setting off currents and rivulets of conflict throughout the society—a pattern of political, economic and social clashes.

Take China, for example. The mass of China's population are peasants living in an essentially First Wave civilization. The initial phases of the Communist revolution were aimed at leading China into the industrial age, and conscious efforts were made to squeeze capital out of the peasantry for investment in industry. All this was done under Soviet tutelage. In short, China was following a Second Wave strategy, trying to spark a traditional industrial revolution. In its first five-year plan, fully 58 per cent of investment was targeted for heavy industry. A wave of industrialization did flow through the society. But it never went very far, and there was violent conflict within the Communist Party and in the population between what might be termed "First Wave" forces who emphasized the need for agricultural development and "Second Wave" industrializers who wanted more steel mills and textile factories, more industry and at a faster rate. Mao's Great Leap Forward campaign, beginning in 1958, and the Soviet pull-out in 1960 symbolized this shift from an industrial to a rural-based approach, from what I would call a Second Wave to a First Wave strategy.

This is, of course, a grand simplification, given the vast complexities of China.

Today in China there is a heated discussion between those who once more wish to follow the path of traditional industrialization—Second Wave development—and many who still, no doubt, favor a First Wave agricultural emphasis. But I suspect there are also now a few who are beginning to explore Third Wave development possibilities which might use high technology to create an advanced economy without compelling the entire country to undergo a massive, disruptive industrial revolution. This introduces a new element into the picture, and creates a new axis around which people will group themselves.

So I see these waves as producing conflict on this macro-level. You can also see evidence of global conflict as different high technology nations—primarily the U.S. and Japan—race to introduce Third Wave industry and capture the new markets associated with it, the software market, for example, based almost entirely on the application of brain power.

And, of course, you can also apply the concepts to conflicts within a single country. For example, in the U.S. we see a political conflict between dying Second Wave regions and expanding Third Wave regions of the country—just compare Detroit and Dallas, for example.

On a still smaller scale, we can see a conflict between industries—the steel and auto industries demand support from Washington; the computer and electronics industries oppose such policies and urge support for the cutting edge industries, instead. One group wants tariff protection, the other demands free trade policy. The same pattern is present in Belgium, France, Germany, Japan and other nations.

Within giant corporations themselves—I visit many of them, and I find there are very often entrenched Second Wave interests battling against newer Third Wave interests. For example, in many large diversified companies, the older part of the company is engaged in mass manufacture and is basically in the business of selling labor. The new parts of the company are in high technology fields, selling increasingly customized products based on a heavy input of brain power. This leads to fundamental internal conflicts over management policies, treatment of the workers, organizational styles, allocations of investment, etc.

And the same sort of thing can be seen in other institutions—old-line school teachers who want rigid, standardizing classroom methods appropriate to a Second Wave world versus new-style educators (usually, though not always, younger) who want to treat each student in a more individualized fashion, want to increase the diversity of courses and methodologies, and want to change the delivery system, itself. In health systems, in energy, in communications, indeed, in almost every field, we can find the same Second Wave versus Third Wave division.

If we ask, in any organization, who lines up behind the Second Wave principles of standardization, centralization, specialization, concentration, and maximization, and who, in general, opposes the application of these principles, we get a fair picture of the Second Wave versus Third Wave line-up.

A similar form of conflict analysis can clarify what is happening not only in industry and education, or in politics, but also with respect to issues like family life, sex roles, race, culture, etc.

When a civilization splits, as it were, when a powerful new wave of associated changes begins to flow through everything from technology and energy systems to family structure and politics, it sets off conflicts within conflicts within conflicts—conflicts at every level of the system.

And when a country, like Brazil, for example, has all three waves of change running through it simultaneously, we can see three concurrent conflict "fronts."

Once we recognize the existence of "wave-fronts," so to speak, that cut across the society, through all classes, races, and groups, we are led to a total reconceptualization of present-day politics—the politics of public life, even the politics within various institutions. These civilizational conflicts form the "super-struggle" within which all the other conflicts in society play themselves out.

That's what I mean by a theory of conflict based on the idea of waves of change.

11 THE ROOTS OF CHANGE

Why are we living through a revolution? Sometimes it appears from the headlines that the earth is caught up in a violent upheaval that can end only in chaos. At other moments, it appears that we are being inexorably drawn toward some highly technological future—that the future is already predetermined and waiting for us, that nothing we can do will change the course of change, itself.

At one end of the spectrum: chance, individual events, surprise, anarchy, uncertainty. At the other: necessity, determinism, broad, sweeping, irresistible historical movements against which no individual can prevail.

Does the individual influence history? And among the many forces that contribute to change, which are predominant? Technology, for example? The economy?

These issues we reserved for our final conversation.

—A.T.

■ Many people who read your work come away with the impression that you are a technological or economic determinist. It sometimes seems that you do regard technology or the economy as key to change. You have various sub-systems nested and entwined with each other, with various characteristic features running through them all. And you see internal fluctuations within each sub-system which, if they happen to amplify one another or to coincide with a major external fluctuation, can cause a major structural change. Nevertheless, you develop these core principles of industrial civilization—standardization for example, or centralization—as more or less emerging from economic requisites.

Even when you address issues of race and sex, it often appears that an economic bias colors your thinking. It is as though your concepts were tempered in an economic furnace. So how do you respond to *this* charge of techno-economic determinism in your work?

□ We've spoken about that before, but it's worth pursuing.

I flatly reject the notion that I am a technological or economic determinist, and anyone reading me closely should be clear on that point. I don't believe any single force drives the system, whether it is technological, economic, sexual, racial or ecological. Different causal forces emerge as salient at different moments, and I think, therefore, that the attempt to find a single dominating causal force is a misguided search for a unique "link that pulls the chain." I simply don't think that way.

I think more in terms of process, interrelationships, rhythms, non-equilibrium, and fields than individual causal vectors; more in terms of mutually interactive open systems, than of one-way causality.

This attitude toward causality is yet another thing that differentiates me from most Marxists. For Marx, the base determines the superstructure. Which translated means that religion, art, ethics, values, law, and culture in general, merely reflect and rationalize class positions, which are, in turn, determined by economic and technological forces.

That's just not how the world works. This division of entire social systems into these two neat categories, with one of them driving or determining the other, is reductionist.

Marx was searching for a single irreducible unit in economics—a kind of atom—out of which he could build a scientific theory of economics, on top of which he could spread, like frosting on the cake, a so-called superstructure. But the science he took as his model was still basically Newtonian. It was pre-Einsteinian. And there is a stifling, closed character to his model, while society, itself, is, if anything, an open system.

Whatever the weaknesses of the Third Wave model—and I would be the last to claim it is all-inclusive and all-revealing—it allows for looser, more complex interactions. It provides a more differentiated picture of social structure. It accepts that technology may sometimes seem to drive the system—but technology, itself, is being continually shaped by other forces.

The technologies a society chooses to focus on are influenced not merely by economic considerations, but by the particular natural resources in that society, by the levels of education, by cultural and even religious taboos, by environmental considerations and the like. That is not a technological determinist's position.

My position stands in marked contrast even to those Marxists who recognize that what they call the superstructure can influence the economic and technological base. For while they admit the possibility of such feed-back, for them the various ideas, laws, values, religions, etc., which comprise the superstructure are themselves merely a reflection of class positions, and those class positions are fundamentally economically determined. Thus there is a tautological character to their argument. One way or another, directly or indirectly, economics and technology drive the entire system—as they see it. That's a position I do not and cannot accept.

■ To rightfully argue that orthodox Marxism is inadequate, in part for being economically determinist, doesn't quite prove that your approach isn't subject to the same criticism. You often show how technology or economics affect other institutions. In *The Third Wave*, for example, you show how the family reacted to changes in the production system. But you rarely make the opposite kind of analysis. You don't show how economic relations, for example, have reacted to changes in family relations.

□ That doesn't mean however, that the family, in turn, didn't alter the economic system. I'm sure it did, and it still does. But it is likely to do so with a lag. Its chief influence is felt, say, 25 years or so down the line. Similarly, education takes the child and has an influence on society. But that influence is muted and felt only at a later stage.

So I believe that in these cases, in the relationship of the economy and the family, for example, the economy is a heavy driving force at first, with the interactions in the other direction delayed for a long period of time. But that doesn't mean I think the "base" determines the "superstructure" or that the economy is an independent variable.

In all my work I have taken pains to show how non-economic factors have influenced the economy. In *Future Shock*, for example, I argued that the speed-up of social and cultural change, among other things, was foreshortening economic relationships, and that growing social and cultural diversity was reorganizing markets. I also have a long section explicitly attacking econo-centrism in planning and government policy-making. So I think the charge of economism is just as unfounded as the charge of technological determinism.

■ In your view, might we not see a strong shift toward Third Wave economic forms, leaving the Second Wave family forms still intact?

□ I don't regard that as likely...

■ It's basically impossible then?

□ I can't say impossible, but I do believe that, when one sphere changes in a social system or civilization, the others are likely to come into accommodation. I believe that this is true, but it is still an assumption. We don't know.

Many years ago William Fielding Ogburn wrote persuasively about cultural lag. He explained what happens when different systems within a society are out of sync with one another. And I think he was right. Different change rates—some of them extremely accelerated—are affecting our social institutions today in wildly varied ways, and the institutions are struggling to adapt to one another's time-pacing. The structure of large-scale business is changing fast. The structure of the schools and the big government bureaucracies is changing more slowly. The society is rapidly differentiating—becoming more diversified. The political system is still geared to low diversity. These lags in adaptation create powerful tensions in society.

But quite apart from the rates and rhythms of change, I assume that, if changes occur in family life or the socio-sphere more generally, there will be accommodative (or resistant) changes elsewhere in the system.

■ And vice versa?

☐ And vice versa, exactly. We are experiencing profound changes in the structure of family life in most of the high tech nations as we move into the Third Wave, and these changes, in turn, affect the economy. On a small scale, for example, the existence of large numbers of singles in our society begins to change the character of the entire housing market. You now find single men buying homes in the suburbs, or you find apartments getting smaller. That, in turn, has obvious economic effects. It is a small example, but there are probably thousands of such effects flowing into the system. There are many others that have not been traced.

For example, as I wrote in 1975, in *The Eco-Spasm Report*, high rates of marriage break-up and re-marriage, geographical mobility and social change generally contribute in an unnoticed way to inflation. I believe they encourage a speed-up in the velocity of money.

The high rate of family break-up has also encouraged the do-it-yourself and self-help movements. These have enormous implications for the future of our economy, only some of which are spelled out in *The Third Wave*. But conventional economists, steeped in the obsolete concepts and vocabulary of the Second Wave era, have scarcely noticed these phenomena. No wonder their forecasts fail so often and their manipulations boomerang.

■ If neither technology nor economics, by themselves, drive the system, then, according to your view, neither does politics. In that case, radical activists of any kind who focus exclusively on politics, or exclusively on any one issue, risk overlooking factors critical to their larger purposes. Treating culture or gender, for example, as peripheral might be the kiss of death, even for the economic or political aims of such groups.

□ Exactly right. There is a phrase, I think from Lenin, about the need to break "the weakest link in the chain." That betrays a notion of social causation that is essentially mechanistic, Second Wave. If one is interested in making—or should we say facilitating—a true revolution, then one is not talking about class replacing class, or about seizing the "state machine" or marching on the Winter Palace. One is talking about something very different and far, far more fundamental—a transformation of the entire civilization. And, if one wishes to help bring that about, focussing exclusively on economic or political factors may be a self-defeating mistake.

It also means that all sorts of people can contribute to that transformation, not simply political activists or "professional revolutionaries." It means that scientists and executives and philosophers and feminists and teachers and nurses and civil rights activists and environmentalists and software designers and all sorts of other people have roles to play, and not just as subordinate legions swept along behind some "vanguard party" or class.

If what I say in *The Third Wave* is right, and the techno-sphere, socio-sphere, info-sphere, bio-sphere, and power-sphere are all related—and that none of these are "base" with all the rest relegated to "superstructure"—then changes are needed in all of them simultaneously. In fact, rapid and profound changes are already occurring in all these spheres, sparked by all sorts of people who would never regard themselves as activists or revolutionaries at all.

CHANCE AND CHANGE

■ You say there is no single future, but an array of possible futures, among which we must choose...

□ Yes, but since the future is not entirely deterministic, there is another facet of this we haven't talked about yet, and that's the element of chance. I believe chance plays a very significant role in social change and I have a very dramatic example.

One day in the spring of 1981, I found myself in the city room of the *Houston Post,* a major daily. I was being interviewed by a reporter, and she was asking me whether the Third Wave is inevitable. I was reeling off what had by then become a stock response: No, I don't believe in historical inevitability. Not only that, I believe that chance plays a considerable role in human affairs. And I suggested that, even as we spoke, some teenager in Guatemala could throw a rock at a soldier and precipitate World War III.

At that instant we heard shots ring out. Three television monitors suddenly clicked on and we heard shouts and cries..."The President's been shot"...and the entire city room ran to the television sets. And there was Haig announcing he was in charge. Lights started flashing, "stop the presses," etc. It was positively spooky, but it takes me back to the relationship between chance and determinism in history.

No, I don't believe that any particular future is necessarily predetermined, and I certainly don't believe that the Third Wave is an inevitability. I'm inclined, once again, to agree with Prigogine. As I understand him, he suggests that both chance and determinism operate—which is not in itself a fresh idea. But Prigogine, I believe, interrelates them in a novel way. What he says, and I'm crudely paraphrasing, is that there comes a moment when, due to whatever fluctuations and pressures, an old structure reaches the point of revolutionary transformation. At that moment, chance operates. The system can go in any number of directions. Then, once that critical next step has been taken, chance has done its job and the system veers in one direction or another, with determinism taking over again until fluctuations produce another crisis of structure.

THE INDIVIDUAL IN HISTORY (AGAIN)

■ Where, in this, is there room for human influence, planning, and organization? Can the individual play a role?

□ Yes, of course. Chance operates. You also have these determined directions. But even in fields that appear to be most determined there is always some give, some room for human influence. At a minimum, our actions can often slow down, divert, resist, or even forestall otherwise likely outcomes. It's possible for someone to cancel the Third Wave instantaneously—through World War III, to use an extreme example. There are all kinds of possibilities that could rewrite the future.

■ Imagine a futurist in Cuba twenty five years ago. Looking around, this person might well have forecast that a future Cuba would look more or less like Guatemala or some other Latin American country today. Or, assuming tremendous foresight, he or she might have read another scenario into the future and foreseen the possibility of revolution and major change. That revolution certainly depended substantially on human activity and intervention. The difference in those two scenarios seems fundamentally to have depended on the revolutionary movement and Castro...

□ Several interpretations are possible. First of all, the point should hardly need to be made that behind the so-called forces of history—

or in terms of my metaphor, the waves of change—stand individuals. "Forces" or "waves" are not things. They must not be reified in the service of some model.

All changes, wars, and advances, all the successes and tragedies of history are made by people, including ordinary people, making decisions, choices.

Castro—and I assume you mean him to stand as a symbol for other revolutionary leaders as well—can be seen as:

1) a chance element. (A man with his energy, drive, intelligence and charisma just happened to be there at a moment when the Batista regime had reached its outer limits, when the fury of the people against Batista was about to peak. Castro, with the same personality and capability, would not have been there had he been born ten years later than he was. Pure chance put Batista and Castro together at the same moment in history.)

2) a partially determined element. (Castro was just one of thousands of babies born in Cuba at the appropriate moment and was shaped into a guerilla leader by the forces of history. In this interpretation, Castro is entirely dispensable. The man or woman rises to the occasion. The external conditions create the charismatic figure when required. If not Castro, someone else.)

3) an insignificant element. (The revolution in Cuba was completely determined by the play of class and other forces, an inevitable struggle. The moment for revolution was a result of a "changed correlation of forces," to use Soviet jargon. And a revolution would have happened with or without Señor Castro. In this case, the larger events in history are pre-determined, and only the minor elements—like people—are left to chance.)

One reasonable way to look at the issue is to combine some of these. Our answer need not be couched in either/or terms. It may well be true that the Batista government had run its course, that it could no longer control the forces seeking its overthrow, that revolution was, so to speak, overdue. Castro grows up during that moment in history, and is, himself, shaped by it. He sees opportunities—for himself as well as for Cuba. At the very moment when the Batista regime is about to topple, it is unclear and subject to chance which way it will fall, who grabs control. But once Castro seizes control (after helping, of course, to accelerate the collapse), the future becomes more sharply determined once more.

I wonder. I still, after all these years, can recall Castro's triumphant visit to Washington and his speech at the National Press Club. I still wonder what shape Cuba might have today if the decision-makers in Washington had offered him economic support rather than unremitting hostility.

So, despite the play of chance, I believe that human intervention is possible. If I chose to be cynical, I could say that, even if human intervention is not effective, we have to behave as though it were. We cannot live happily as human beings in the belief that our own actions don't matter.

AN APPETITE FOR SURREALISM

■ And what about you? Does that apply to you as well? Do you need the illusion or the reality of "mattering" to keep you happy?

□ Yes, mattering matters.

But that shouldn't be taken too literally. We live in a world filled with cruelty, sorrow and anger, along with radiant promise, and the only way to survive, as we transit through it, is with a sense of humor and an appetite for surrealism.

We need to recognize that we are all part of a fantastic cosmic wisecrack—and still glory in it, enjoy the joke, laugh at it and at ourselves.

I wrote and wrote and wrote long before there was anyone to read it. I write, yes, to persuade people of what I think is morally and intellectually right. But also because the very process of writing changes *me*. It clarifies my thoughts. It organizes my time and my life. I write because not to do so leaves me empty and dissatisfied.

I write because when I succeed in glimpsing some previously unnoticed pattern in the swirling, seeming chaos around us, and am able to convey that fresh insight to my readers, I feel a tiny touch of what the Spanish explorer felt on first seeing the Pacific, standing upon that "peak in Darien."

INDEX